1 603 1987

LANGUAGE ARTS 700
Teacher's Guide

Author:
Alpha Omega Publications

Editor:
Alan Christopherson, M.S.

Alpha Omega
PUBLICATIONS

804 N. 2nd Ave. E.
Rock Rapids, IA 51246-1759

LANGUAGE ARTS 700

LIFEPAC® Overview

LANGUAGE ARTS SCOPE & SEQUENCE

KINDERGARTEN

Lessons 1-40	Lessons 41-80	Lessons 81-120	Lessons 121-160
Alphabet -say the alphabet **Colors** -recognize colors **Directions** -left to right **Following directions** -oral and written **Grammar** -form simple sentences **Listening skills** **Personal recognition** -read and write first name -know age and address -recognize names of family members **Phonics** -short *a, e, i* vowels -initial: *b, t, m, r, s, n, d, p, l* -form and read simple words -form rhyming words **Shapes** -circle, square, triangle, and rectangle -recognize shapes in objects **Stories and poems** -create simple stories and poems **Writing** -form circle and lines -*Aa, Bb, Dd, Ee, Ii, Ll, Mm, Nn, Pp, Rr, Ss,* and *Tt*	**Grammar** -sentences begin with capital, end with period **Patterns** -simple shape, color patterns **Personal recognition** -read and write first and last name **Phonics** -*short a, e, i, o,* and *u* vowels -initial: *k, c, ck, f, h, g, j, v, w, y, z, qu,* and *x* -read simple sentences **Position/direction concepts** -in/out, in front of/behind, up/down, on/off, open/closed, over/under **Sequencing** -alphabetical order -simple story **Shapes** -oval **Size concepts** -big/little, large/small **Writing** -*Kk, Cc, Ff, Hh, Oo, Gg, Jj, Vv, Ww, Uu, Yy, Zz, Qq,* and *Xx*	**Phonics** -recognize the short vowel sounds -recognize all initial consonant sounds -recognize long *a, e, i, o,* and *u* sounds -silent *e* -initial consonant digraphs: *sh, ch,* both soft and hard *th* -final consonant sounds: *_b, _ck, _k, _l* **Word recognition** -color words, number words, and shape words **Writing** -name -complete alphabet, capital and small letters -all color words -number words: *one, two, three, four, five, six* -shape words: *circle, square, triangle*	**Phonics** -recognize the long vowel sounds -initial consonant digraphs: *wh,* review *ch, sh, th* -recognize all final consonant sounds **Stories and poems** -create, tell, and recite stories and poems **Word recognition** -position/direction words: *up/down, high/low, in/inside, out/outside, top/bottom* -number words: *seven, eight, nine, ten* -shape words: *rectangle, oval, star* **Writing** -number words: *seven, eight, nine, ten* -shape words: *rectangle, oval, star* -position/direction words: *up/down, high/low, in/inside, out/outside, top/bottom*

LANGUAGE ARTS SCOPE & SEQUENCE

	Alphabet Sounds (Grade 1)	The Parts of Speech (Grade 2)	Reading Skills (Grade 3)
Unit 1	**ALPHABET AND SHORT VOWEL SOUNDS** • Short vowel sounds • Consonants • Main ideas • Rhyming words	**KNOW YOUR NOUNS** • Review vowels and consonants • Beginning, middle, and ending sounds • Singular and plural nouns • Common and proper nouns	**OLD AND NEW SKILLS** • Vowels and consonants • Sentence phrases • Capital letters • Reading skills
Unit 2	**RHYMING WORDS, ADDING "ING"** • Kinds of sentences • Cardinal and ordinal numbers • Suffixes and plurals • Classifying	**ACTION VERBS** • Vowel digraphs • Action words - verbs • Following directions • The dictionary • ABC order	**BUILDING WORDS AND SENTENCES** • Long and short vowels • Questions • ABC order • Capital letters
Unit 3	**CONSONANT DIGRAPHS, SOFT C AND G** • Consonant digraphs • Compounds and syllables • Possessives and contractions • Soft c and g	**SIMPLE SENTENCES** • R-controlled vowels • Consonant blends • Using capital letters • Subjects and verbs in sentences	**WORDS: GETTING TO THE ROOTS** • Root words • Dictionary guide words • Synonyms and antonyms • Capital letters
Unit 4	**VERBS, BLENDS, AND SILENT LETTERS** • Paragraphs • Silent letters • Sequencing • Subject-verb agreement	**TYPES OF SENTENCES** • Consonant digraphs • Statement, question, and exclamatory sentences • Using capital letters • The library	**WORDS: HOW TO USE THEM** • Noun and verb • Adjective and adverb • Irregular vowels • Composition
Unit 5	**LONG VOWELS AND SYLLABLES** • Long vowels and homonyms • Syllables, possessives, and contractions • Plurals and suffixes • Poetry	**USING PUNCTUATION** • Diphthongs • Punctuation review • Contractions • Rules for making words plural • Writing a biography	**SENTENCE: START TO FINISH** • Main idea • Capital letters and punctuation • Paragraphs • Making words plural
Unit 6	**R-CONTROLLED VOWELS AND PLURALS** • R-controlled vowels • Writing stories • Pronouns • Following directions	**ADJECTIVES** • Rhyming words • Biblical poetry • Synonyms and antonyms • Adjectives in sentences • Comparative and superlative adjectives	**ALL ABOUT BOOKS** • Main idea • Books • Stories • Poems • Critical thinking
Unit 7	**VOWEL DIGRAPHS AND SENTENCES** • Vowel digraphs • Letters — business, friendly, invitations • Syllables	**POSSESSIVE NOUNS** • Introduction to letter writing • Pronunciation key • Possessive nouns • Silent consonants • Homonyms	**READING AND WRITING** • For directions • Friendly letters • Pronouns • Fact and fiction
Unit 8	**VOWEL DIGRAPHS AND POSSESSIVES** • Vowel digraphs • Subject-verb agreement • Compounds and contractions • Possessives • Pronoun	**PRONOUNS** • Author's intent and use of titles • Predicting content • Character, setting, and plot • Analogies • Writing in cursive	**READING SKILLS** • For sequence • For detail • Being and compound verbs • Drama
Unit 9	**DIPHTHONGS AND CONTRACTIONS** • Vowel digraphs • Titles and main ideas • Sentences and paragraphs • Proper nouns	**VERB TYPES AND TENSES** • Review action verbs • Dividing words into syllables • State of being verbs • Past and present verb tenses	**MORE READING AND WRITING** • For information • Thank-you letters • Book reports • Reference books
Unit 10	**PHONICS AND GRAMMAR REVIEW** • Letters and sounds • Contractions • Plurals and possessives • Sentences • Stories	**LOOKING BACK** • Nouns and verbs • Word division • Consonant blends and digraphs • Prefixes, suffixes, and root words • Possessives, pronouns, and adjectives	**LOOKING BACK** • Reading for comprehension • Sentence punctuation • Writing letters • Parts of speech

LANGUAGE ARTS SCOPE & SEQUENCE

Written Communication and Fiction (Grade 4)	Story Elements and Poetry (Grade 5)	Reading for a Purpose (Grade 6)	
WRITTEN COMMUNICATION • Word derivations • Story sequence • Writing an outline • Writing a report	**STORY MESSAGES** • Main idea and plot • Character and setting • Dialogue • Diphthongs • Digraphs	**READING FOR A PURPOSE** • Critical thinking • Research data • Parables • Synonyms	Unit 1
SOUNDS TO WORDS • Hard and soft — c and g • Parts of a dictionary • Accented syllables • Haiku poetry	**MAIN IDEAS** • Poetry and stories • Synonyms • Topic sentences • Adjectives and nouns • Compounds	**FORMING NEW WORDS** • Prefixes and suffixes • Synonyms and antonyms • Adjectives and adverbs • Critical thinking	Unit 2
WORDS: HOW TO USE THEM • Prefixes and suffixes • Homonyms and antonyms • Poetry and stories • Writing an outline	**WORDS TO STORIES** • Subject and predicate • Adverbs • Critical thinking • Writing a short story • Idioms	**BETTER READING** • Story elements • Author's purpose • Information sources • Outline	Unit 3
MORE WORDS: HOW TO USE THEM • Parts of speech • Written directions • Verb tenses • Possessives	**WRITTEN REPORT** • Outline • Metaphor and simile • Writing the report • Types of sentences	**SENTENCES** • Capitals and punctuation • Author's purpose • Propaganda • Types of sentences	Unit 4
WRITING FOR CLARITY • Figures of speech • Capital letters • Punctuation marks • Writing stories	**STORY ELEMENTS** • Legend • Dialogue and quotations • Word order and usage • Story elements • Implied meaning	**READING SKILLS** • Following directions • Literary forms • Phrases, nouns, and verbs • Paragraph structure	Unit 5
FUN WITH FICTION • Book reports • Fiction and nonfiction • Parables and fables • Poetry	**POETRY** • Rhythm • Symbolism • Personification • Irregular plurals • Stanza	**POETRY** • Similes and metaphors • Alliteration and homonyms • Palindromes • Figures of speech • Acronyms	Unit 6
FACT AND FICTION • Nouns and verbs • Contractions • Biography • Tall tales • Fables	**WORD USAGE** • Common, plural, and possessive nouns • Fact and opinion • Story and main idea	**STORIES** • Story elements • Nouns and pronouns • Vowel digraphs • Business letters	Unit 7
GRAMMAR AND WRITING • Adjectives to compare • Adverbs • Figurative language • Paragraphs	**ALL ABOUT VERBS** • Tense and action • Participles • Regular and irregular • Singular and plural	**ANALYZING THE NEWS** • Propaganda • News stories • Auxiliary verbs and verb tenses • Adverbs	Unit 8
THE WRITTEN REPORT • Planning a report • Finding information • Creating an outline • Writing a report	**READING FLUENCY** • Speed reading • Graphic aids • Study skills • Literary forms	**READING THE BIBLE** • Parables and proverbs • Hebrew poetry and prophecy • Bible history • Old Testament law	Unit 9
LOOKING BACK • Reading skills • Nouns and adverbs • Written communication • Literary forms	**LOOKING BACK** • Literary forms • Parts of speech • Writing skills • Study skills	**LOOKING BACK** • Literary forms • Writing letters • Parts of speech • Punctuation	Unit 10

LANGUAGE ARTS SCOPE & SEQUENCE

	Grammar and Nonfiction (Grade 7)	Speaking and Writing Skills (Grade 8)	English I (Grade 9)
Unit 1	**WORD USAGE** • Proper and common nouns • Pronouns • Prefixes and suffixes • Synonyms and antonyms	**IMPROVING COMMUNICATION** • Roots and inflections • Affixes and interjections • Oral and written directions • Non-verbal communication	**THE STRUCTURE OF LANGUAGE** • Nouns, adjectives, and prepositions • Verbs, adverbs, and conjunctions • Sentence parts • Diagram sentences
Unit 2	**MORE WORD USAGE** • Speech: Stress and pitch • Verb tenses • Principle parts	**ALL ABOUT ENGLISH** • Origin of language • Classification of nouns, pronouns, verbs, adjectives, and adverbs	**NATURE OF LANGUAGE** • Origin of language • Using oral and written language • Dictionary • Writing a paper
Unit 3	**BIOGRAPHIES** • Biography as a form • Flashback technique • Deductive reasoning • Base and root words	**PUNCTUATION AND LITERATURE** • Connecting and interrupting • The essay • Thesis statement	**PRACTICAL ENGLISH** • Dictionary use • Mnemonics • Writing a paper • Five-minute speech
Unit 4	**STRUCTURE OF LANGUAGE** • Verb tenses • Principle parts • Sentence creativity • Speech: Pitch and accent	**WORDS AND HOW TO USE THEM** • Dictionary • Thesaurus • Accent and diacritical marks • Standard and nonstandard	**SHORT STORY FUNDAMENTALS** • Plot and setting • Characterization • Conflict • Symbolism
Unit 5	**THE NATURE OF ENGLISH** • Formal and informal • Redundant expressions • Verb tenses • Subject-verb agreement	**CORRECT LANGUAGE USAGE** • Using good form • Synonyms and antonyms • Homonyms • Good speaking qualities	**LANGUAGE IN LITERATURE** • Collective nouns and verbs • Use of comparisons • Gerunds and participles • Literary genres
Unit 6	**THE MECHANICS OF ENGLISH** • Punctuation • Complements and modifiers • Subordinate and coordinate clauses	**LANGUAGE AND LITERATURE** • History of English • Coordination and Subordination • Autobiography	**MEANING IN POETRY AND PROSE** • Author's purpose and meaning • Meaning of structure • Factors of persuasion • Understanding poetry
Unit 7	**THE HIDING PLACE: A STUDY GUIDE** • Sequence of events • Facts about characters • Author's purpose • Character sketch	**CRITICAL READING AND PARAGRAPH SKILLS** • Word evaluation • The paragraph: Structure, coherence, introduction, and conclusion	**COMMUNICATION** • Planning a speech • Listening comprehension • Business, informal, and social letters
Unit 8	**LITERATURE** • Nonfiction • Listening skills • Commas and semicolons • Nonverbal communication	**WRITING, LISTENING, AND READING** • Business letters • Personal letters • Four steps to listening • Nonfiction	**LIBRARY AND DRAMA** • Library resources • Drama: History, elements, and reading • *The Miracle Worker*
Unit 9	**COMPOSITIONS** • Sentence types • Quality of paragraphs • Pronunciation • Nonsense literature	**SPEAK AND WRITE** • Etymology • Modifiers • Number and tense • Oral report	**STUDIES IN THE NOVEL** • History and definition • Critical essay • *Twenty Thousand Leagues Under the Sea*
Unit 10	**LOOKING BACK** • Parts of speech • Sentence structure • Punctuation • How to communicate	**LANGUAGE ELEMENTS IN REVIEW** • Composition structure • Parts of speech • Critical thinking • Literary forms	**LOOKING BACK** • Communication: Writing, speaking, and listening • Using resources • Literature review • Diagram sentences

LANGUAGE ARTS SCOPE & SEQUENCE

English II (Grade 10)	English III (Grade 11)	English IV (Grade 12)	
THE DEVELOPMENT OF ENGLISH • Historical development • Varieties of English • Substandard and standard • Changes in English	STANDARD ENGLISH • Need for standard English • Guardians of the standard • Dictionaries • Types of standard English texts	THE WORTH OF WORDS • Word categories • Expository writing • Sentence structure • Diction	Unit 1
LISTENING AND SPEAKING • Noun plurals • Suffixes • Creating a speech • Nature of listening	WRITING EFFECTIVE SENTENCES • Subordinate clauses and conjunctions • Relative pronouns • Verbals • Appositives	THE STRUCTURE OF LANGUAGE • Parts of speech • Sentence structure • Subordinate phrases • Subordinate clauses	Unit 2
WRITING EFFECTIVE SENTENCES • Participles and infinitives • Prepositions and gerunds • Simple, compound, and complex sentences • Diagram sentences	CLEAR CONNECTIONS: A WRITING WORKSHOP • Understanding pronouns • Using pronouns correctly • Using modifiers correctly • Parallel sentence structures	READ, RESEARCH, AND LISTEN • Reading skills • Resources for research • Taking notes • Drawing conclusions	Unit 3
THE POWER OF WORDS • Etymology • Poetic devices • Literal, figurative, and symbolic poetry • Connotations	WHY STUDY READING? • Greek and Latin roots • Diacritical markings • Finding the main idea • Analyzing a textbook	THE GIFT OF LANGUAGE • Biblical origin • Koine Greek • Purpose of grammar • Semantics	Unit 4
ELEMENTS OF COMPOSITION • Paragraphs • Connectives and transitions • Elements and ideas of expository writing	POETRY • Metrical feet and sets • Musical effects • Universality • Imagery • Connotation	MEDIEVAL ENGLISH LITERATURE • Early England • Medieval England • Fourteenth century • Chaucer	Unit 5
STRUCTURE AND READING • Subordinate clauses • Pronouns: Gender, case, and agreement • Reading for recognition	NONFICTION • Elements • Essays, diaries, newspapers, and biographies • Composition	ELIZABETHAN LITERATURE • Poetry • Prose • Drama • Essay	Unit 6
ORAL READING AND DRAMA • Skills of oral reading • Drama: History, irony, elements, and allegory • *Everyman*	AMERICAN DRAMA • Development and history • Structure • Purpose • *Our Town*	17TH AND 18TH CENTURY ENGLISH LITERATURE • Historical background • Puritan literature • Common sense and satire • Sensibility	Unit 7
THE SHORT STORY • Elements • Enjoying short stories • Writing • The literary critique	STUDIES IN THE AMERICAN NOVEL • Eighteenth, nineteenth, and twentieth century • *The Old Man and the Sea* • The critical essay	CREATIVE WRITING • Fundamentals • Inspiration • Technique and style • Form and process	Unit 8
THE NOVEL • Elements • *In His Steps* • The critical essay • The book review	RESEARCH • Using sources • Stating the thesis • Outline • Writing the paper	ROMANTIC AND VICTORIAN POETRY • Wordsworth and Coleridge • Gordon, Byron, and Shelley • Keats, Tennyson, and Hopkins • Robert and Elizabeth B. Browning	Unit 9
LOOKING BACK • Writing skills • Speech skills • Poetry • Short stories and novels • Drama	REVIEWING COMMUNICATION SKILLS AND LITERATURE • Analyzing written word • Effective sentences • Expository prose • Genres of American literature	LANGUAGE AND ENGLISH LITERATURE REVIEW • Creative writing • English literature: Medieval to Victorian	Unit 10

STRUCTURE OF THE LIFEPAC CURRICULUM

The LIFEPAC curriculum is conveniently structured to provide one Teacher's Guide containing teacher support material with answer keys and ten student worktexts for each subject at grade levels 2 through 12. The worktext format of the LIFEPACs allows the student to read the textual information and complete workbook activities all in the same booklet. The easy-to-follow LIFEPAC numbering system lists the grade as the first number(s) and the last two digits as the number of the series. For example, the Language Arts LIFEPAC at the 6th grade level, 5th book in the series would be LAN0605.

Each LIFEPAC is divided into three to five sections and begins with an introduction or overview of the booklet as well as a series of specific learning objectives to give a purpose to the study of the LIFEPAC. The introduction and objectives are followed by a vocabulary section which may be found at the beginning of each section at the lower levels or in the glossary at the high school level. Vocabulary words are used to develop word recognition and should not be confused with the spelling words introduced later in the LIFEPAC. The student should learn all vocabulary words before working the LIFEPAC sections to improve comprehension, retention, and reading skills.

Each activity or written assignment in grades 2 through 12 has a number for easy identification, such as 1.1. The first number corresponds to the LIFEPAC section and the number to the right of the decimal is the number of the activity.

Teacher checkpoints, which are essential to maintain quality learning, are found at various locations throughout the LIFEPAC.

The teacher should check:
1) neatness of work and penmanship,
2) quality of understanding (tested with a short oral quiz),
3) thoroughness of answers (complete sentences and paragraphs, correct spelling, etc.),
4) completion of activities (no blank spaces), and
5) accuracy of answers as compared to the answer key (all answers correct).

The self test questions in grades 2 through 12 are also number coded for easy reference. For example, 2.015 means that this is the 15th question in the self test of Section 2. The first number corresponds to the LIFEPAC section, the zero indicates that it is a self test question, and the number to the right of the zero the question number.

The LIFEPAC test is packaged at the center of each LIFEPAC. It should be removed and put aside before giving the booklet to the student for study.

Answer and test keys in grades 2 through 12 have the same numbering system as the LIFEPACs. The student may be given access to the answer keys (not the test keys) under teacher supervision so that he can score his own work.

A thorough study of the LIFEPAC Scope & Sequence by the teacher before instruction begins is essential to the success of the student. The teacher should become familiar with expected skill mastery and understand how these grade-level skills fit into the overall skill development of the curriculum. The teacher should also preview the objectives that appear at the beginning of each LIFEPAC for additional preparation and planning.

TEST SCORING AND GRADING

Answer keys and test keys give examples of correct answers. They convey the idea, but the student may use many ways to express a correct answer. The teacher should check for the essence of the answer, not for the exact wording. Many questions are high level and require thinking and creativity on the part of the student. Each answer should be scored based on whether or not the main idea written by the student matches the model example. "Any Order" or "Either Order" in a key indicates that no particular order is necessary to be correct.

Most self tests and LIFEPAC tests at the lower elementary levels are scored at 1 point per answer; however, the upper levels may have a point system awarding 2 to 5 points for various answers or questions. Further, the total test points will vary; they may not always equal 100 points. They may be 78, 85, 100, 105, etc.

Example 1

Example 2

A score box similar to ex. 1 above is located at the end of each self test and on the front of the LIFEPAC test. The bottom score, 72, represents the total number of points possible on the test. The upper score, 58, represents the number of points your student will need to receive an 80% or passing grade. If you wish to establish the exact percentage that your student has achieved, find the total points of his correct answers and divide it by the bottom number (in this case 72).
For example, if your student has a point total of 65, divide 65 by 72 for a grade of 90%. Referring to ex. 2, on a test with a total of 105 possible points, the student would have to receive a minimum of 84 correct points for an 80% or passing grade. If your student has received 93 points, simply divide the 93 by 105 for a percentage grade of 89%. Students who receive a score below 80% should review the LIFEPAC and retest using the appropriate Alternate Test found in the Teacher's Guide.

The following is a guideline to assign letter grades for completed LIFEPACs based on a maximum total score of 100 points.

Example:

LIFEPAC Test	=	60% of the Total Score (or percent grade)
Self Test	=	25% of the Total Score (average percent of self tests)
Reports	=	10% or 10* points per LIFEPAC
Oral Work	=	5% or 5* points per LIFEPAC

*Determined by the teacher's subjective evaluation of the student's daily work.

Example:

LIFEPAC Test Score	=	92%	92 x .60 = 55	points
Self Test Average	=	90%	90 x .25 = 23	points
Reports			= 8	points
Oral Work			= 4	points

TOTAL POINTS	= 90 points

Grade Scale based on point system:

100 – 94	=	A
93 – 86	=	B
85 – 77	=	C
76 – 70	=	D
Below 70	=	F

TEACHER HINTS AND STUDYING TECHNIQUES

LIFEPAC activities are written to check the level of understanding of the preceding text. The student may look back to the text as necessary to complete these activities; however, a student should never attempt to do the activities without reading (studying) the text first. Self tests and LIFEPAC tests are never open book tests.

Language arts activities (skill integration) often appear within other subject curriculum. The purpose is to give the student an opportunity to test his skill mastery outside of the context in which it was presented.

Writing complete answers (paragraphs) to some questions is an integral part of the LIFEPAC curriculum in all subjects. This builds communication and organization skills, increases understanding and retention of ideas, and helps enforce good penmanship. Complete sentences should be encouraged for this type of activity. Obviously, single words or phrases do not meet the intent of the activity, since multiple lines are given for the response.

Review is essential to student success. Time invested in review where review is suggested will be time saved in correcting errors later. Self tests, unlike the section activities, are closed book. This procedure helps to identify weaknesses before they become too great to overcome. Certain objectives from self tests are cumulative and test previous sections; therefore, good preparation for a self test must include all material studied up to that testing point.

The following procedure checklist has been found to be successful in developing good study habits in the LIFEPAC curriculum.

1. Read the introduction and Table of Contents.
2. Read the objectives.
3. Recite and study the entire vocabulary (glossary) list.
4. Study each section as follows:
   a. Read the introduction and study the section objectives.
   b. Read all the text for the entire section, but answer none of the activities.
   c. Return to the beginning of the section and memorize each vocabulary word and definition.
   d. Reread the section, complete the activities, check the answers with the answer key, correct all errors, and have the teacher check.
   e. Read the self test but do not answer the questions.
   f. Go to the beginning of the first section and reread the text and answers to the activities up to the self test you have not yet done.
   g. Answer the questions to the self test without looking back.
   h. Have the self test checked by the teacher.
   i. Correct the self test and have the teacher check the corrections.
   j. Repeat steps a–i for each section.
5. Use the SQ3R method to prepare for the LIFEPAC test.

   Scan the whole LIFEPAC.
   Question yourself on the objectives.
   Read the whole LIFEPAC again.
   Recite through an oral examination.
   Review weak areas.

6. Take the LIFEPAC test as a closed book test.
7. LIFEPAC tests are administered and scored under direct teacher supervision. Students who receive scores below 80% should review the LIFEPAC using the SQ3R study method and take the Alternate Test located in the Teacher's Guide. The final test grade may be the grade on the Alternate Test or an average of the grades from the original LIFEPAC test and the Alternate Test.

GOAL SETTING AND SCHEDULES

Each school must develop its own schedule, because no single set of procedures will fit every situation. The following is an example of a daily schedule that includes the five LIFEPAC subjects as well as time slotted for special activities.

Possible Daily Schedule

8:15 – 8:25	Pledges, prayer, songs, devotions, etc.
8:25 – 9:10	Bible
9:10 – 9:55	Language Arts
9:55 – 10:15	Recess (juice break)
10:15 – 11:00	Math
11:00 – 11:45	History & Geography
11:45 – 12:30	Lunch, recess, quiet time
12:30 – 1:15	Science
1:15 –	Drill, remedial work, enrichment*

***Enrichment**: Computer time, physical education, field trips, fun reading, games and puzzles, family business, hobbies, resource persons, guests, crafts, creative work, electives, music appreciation, projects.*

Basically, two factors need to be considered when assigning work to a student in the LIFEPAC curriculum.

The first is time. An average of 45 minutes should be devoted to each subject, each day. Remember, this is only an average. Because of extenuating circumstances, a student may spend only 15 minutes on a subject one day and the next day spend 90 minutes on the same subject.

The second factor is the number of pages to be worked in each subject. A single LIFEPAC is designed to take three to four weeks to complete. Allowing about three to four days for LIFEPAC introduction, review, and tests, the student has approximately 15 days to complete the LIFEPAC pages. Simply take the number of pages in the LIFEPAC, divide it by 15 and you will have the number of pages that must be completed on a daily basis to keep the student on schedule. For example, a LIFEPAC containing 45 pages will require three completed pages per day. Again, this is only an average. While working a 45-page LIFEPAC, the student may complete only one page the first day if the text has a lot of activities or reports, but go on to complete five pages the next day.

Long-range planning requires some organization. Because the traditional school year originates in the early fall of one year and continues to late spring of the following year, a calendar should be devised that covers this period of time. Approximate beginning and completion dates can be noted on the calendar as well as special occasions such as holidays, vacations and birthdays. Since each LIFEPAC takes three to four weeks or 18 days to complete, it should take about 180 school days to finish a set of ten LIFEPACs. Starting at the beginning school date, mark off 18 school days on the calendar and that will become the targeted completion date for the first LIFEPAC. Continue marking the calendar until you have established dates for the remaining nine LIFEPACs making adjustments for previously noted holidays and vacations. If all five subjects are being used, the ten established target dates should be the same for the LIFEPACs in each subject.

TEACHING SUPPLEMENTS

The sample weekly lesson plan and student grading sheet forms are included in this section as teacher support materials and may be duplicated at the convenience of the teacher.

The student grading sheet is provided for those who desire to follow the suggested guidelines for assignment of letter grades as previously discussed. The student's self test scores should be posted as percentage grades. When the LIFEPAC is completed the teacher should average the self test grades, multiply the average by .25 and post the points in the box marked self test points. The LIFEPAC percentage grade should be multiplied by .60 and posted. Next, the teacher should award and post points for written reports and oral work. A report may be any type of written work assigned to the student whether it is a LIFEPAC or additional learning activity. Oral work includes the student's ability to respond orally to questions which may or may not be related to LIFEPAC activities or any type of oral report assigned by the teacher. The points may then be totaled and a final grade entered along with the date that the LIFEPAC was completed.

The Student Record Book, which was specifically designed for use with the Alpha Omega curriculum, provides space to record weekly progress for one student over a nine-week period as well as a place to post self test and LIFEPAC scores. The Student Record Books are available through the current Alpha Omega catalog; however, unlike the enclosed forms, these books are not for duplication and should be purchased in sets of four to cover a full academic year.

This section of the language arts Teacher's Guide also includes a *Book Report Form* and *Books Read Chart*. The *Book Report Form* and the *Books Read Chart* may be duplicated for individual student use.

The Index of Concepts is a quick reference guide for the teacher who may be looking for a rule or explanation that applies to a particular concept. It does not identify each use of the concept in the various LIFEPACs. The concepts change by grade level with the emphasis on phonics and reading skills for younger students changing to spelling and grammar for the older students.

WEEKLY LESSON PLANNER

Week of:

	Subject	Subject	Subject	Subject
Monday				
Tuesday				
Wednesday				
Thursday				
Friday				

WEEKLY LESSON PLANNER

Week of:

	Subject	Subject	Subject	Subject
Monday				
Tuesday				
Wednesday				
Thursday				
Friday				

Student Name _____   Year _____

Bible

LP	Self Test Scores by Sections					Self Test Points	LIFEPAC Test	Oral Points	Report Points	Final Grade	Date
	1	2	3	4	5						
01											
02											
03											
04											
05											
06											
07											
08											
09											
10											

History & Geography

LP	Self Test Scores by Sections					Self Test Points	LIFEPAC Test	Oral Points	Report Points	Final Grade	Date
	1	2	3	4	5						
01											
02											
03											
04											
05											
06											
07											
08											
09											
10											

Language Arts

LP	Self Test Scores by Sections					Self Test Points	LIFEPAC Test	Oral Points	Report Points	Final Grade	Date
	1	2	3	4	5						
01											
02											
03											
04											
05											
06											
07											
08											
09											
10											

Student Name _____   Year _____

Math

LP	Self Test Scores by Sections					Self Test Points	LIFEPAC Test	Oral Points	Report Points	Final Grade	Date
	1	2	3	4	5						
01											
02											
03											
04											
05											
06											
07											
08											
09											
10											

Science

LP	Self Test Scores by Sections					Self Test Points	LIFEPAC Test	Oral Points	Report Points	Final Grade	Date
	1	2	3	4	5						
01											
02											
03											
04											
05											
06											
07											
08											
09											
10											

Spelling/Electives

LP	Self Test Scores by Sections					Self Test Points	LIFEPAC Test	Oral Points	Report Points	Final Grade	Date
	1	2	3	4	5						
01											
02											
03											
04											
05											
06											
07											
08											
09											
10											

BOOK REPORT FORM

Title _____   Your Name _____

Author _____   Date _____

Illustrator _____   Principal Characters _____

Number of Pages _____   _____

Copyright Date _____   _____

Fiction or Nonfiction _____   Setting _____

Summary: A summary gives the important events of a story or book. It skips most of the details but a few make the report more interesting. The summary should be written in complete sentences.

_____

_____

_____

_____

_____

_____

_____

_____

_____

_____

_____

_____

_____

Tell why you did or did not like the book.

_____

_____

_____

_____

_____

_____

_____

Name: _____

Books Read

Title:	Title:	Title:	Title:
Author:	Author:	Author:	Author:
Date:	Date:	Date:	Date:
Title:	Title:	Title:	Title:
Author:	Author:	Author:	Author:
Date:	Date:	Date:	Date:
Title:	Title:	Title:	Title:
Author:	Author:	Author:	Author:
Date:	Date:	Date:	Date:
Title:	Title:	Title:	Title:
Author:	Author:	Author:	Author:
Date:	Date:	Date:	Date:
Title:	Title:	Title:	Title:
Author:	Author:	Author:	Author:
Date:	Date:	Date:	Date:
Title:	Title:	Title:	Title:
Author:	Author:	Author:	Author:
Date:	Date:	Date:	Date:
Title:	Title:	Title:	Title:
Author:	Author:	Author:	Author:
Date:	Date:	Date:	Date:
Title:	Title:	Title:	Title:
Author:	Author:	Author:	Author:
Date:	Date:	Date:	Date:
Title:	Title:	Title:	Title:
Author:	Author:	Author:	Author:
Date:	Date:	Date:	Date:

LANGUAGE ARTS 700 INDEX OF CONCEPTS

INSTRUCTIONS FOR LANGUAGE ARTS

The LIFEPAC curriculum from grades 2 through 12 is structured so that the daily instructional material is written directly into the LIFEPACs. The student is encouraged to read and follow this instructional material in order to develop independent study habits. The teacher should introduce the LIFEPAC to the student, set a required completion schedule, complete teacher checks, be available for questions regarding both content and procedures, administer and grade tests, and develop additional learning activities as desired. Teachers working with several students may schedule their time so that students are assigned to a quiet work activity when it is necessary to spend instructional time with one particular student.

Language arts includes those subjects that develop students' communication skills. The LIFEPAC approach to combining reading, spelling, penmanship, composition, grammar, speech and literature in a single unit allows the teacher to integrate the study of these various language arts subject areas. The variety and scope of the curriculum may make it difficult for students to complete the required material within the suggested daily scheduled time of 45 minutes. Spelling, book reports and various forms of composition may need to be completed during the afternoon enrichment period.

Cursive handwriting is introduced in the second grade LIFEPAC 208, with regular practice following in subsequent LIFEPACs. Diacritical markings are defined in the third grade LIFEPAC 304. A pronunciation key including diacritical markings is provided after the vocabulary word lists in all subjects beginning with LIFEPAC 305.

This section of the language arts Teacher's Guide includes the following teacher aids for each unit: Suggested and Required Material (supplies), Additional Learning Activities, Answer Keys, Alternate LIFEPAC Tests, and LIFEPAC Spelling Tests.

Spelling tests contained in the Teacher's Guide are final spelling tests and should be administered with each Language Arts LIFEPAC test. Many words such as "piece" and "peace" are dependent on meaning for correct spelling. By placing the spelling words in sentences, the spelling tests simplify the teacher's work of properly presenting the correct words from the LIFEPAC spelling lists. The practice spelling tests in each section of each LIFEPAC should be designed by the teacher and are not included in this Guide.

The materials section refers only to LIFEPAC materials and does not include materials which may be needed for the additional learning activities. Additional learning activities provide a change from the daily school routine, encourage the students' interest in learning and may be used as a reward for good study habits.

LANGUAGE ARTS 701

Unit 1: Word Usage

TEACHER NOTES

MATERIALS NEEDED FOR LIFEPAC	
Required	Suggested
None	• King James Version of the Bible • Roget's *Thesaurus of Synonyms and Antonyms* • dictionary • reference books or online sources

ADDITIONAL LEARNING ACTIVITIES

Section 1: Labeling with Nouns

1. Discussion questions:

    a. What do all the languages in the world have in common?

    b. Why do we need labels for food?

    c. How did God stop work on the Tower of Babel?

    d. Why couldn't they continue to work?

    e. What are synonyms?

    f. What are dialects?

    g. Where can you find many synonyms and antonyms?

    h. What is a category?

    i. What do we mean by a common noun?

    j. What do we mean by a proper noun?

    k. Where can we find the origin of names?

    l. What is a digraph?

2. To make this game, get a large piece of cardboard or posterboard, and cut a circle about two or three feet in diameter. (You can also use backing cardboard from many kinds of pizzas.) Write a number of prefixes or suffixes around the edge of a circle. You can change the face of the circle by using extra overlap of paper if you want to do so. Then make a spinner. Put the spinner in the center of the circle with some kind of fastener. Make word cards for base or root words. Give an equal number of word cards to each student. Several can play the game. Each student spins the pointer. The group leader calls on each student and has him try to attach the prefix or suffix to the top card on his pile. The student should also pronounce the word he has formed by adding the prefix or suffix. The first student to get all his cards in the box wins.

3. Have a student look up information on the Morse code and make an oral or written report.

Section 2: Using Pronouns

1. Discussion questions:

   a. What are personal pronouns?

   b. What do first person pronouns do?

   c. When do you use a second person pronoun?

   d. When should you use a third person pronoun?

   e. What would happen if we didn't have personal pronouns?

   f. What are nominative pronouns?

   g. What does a pronoun follow when used as a predicative nominative?

   h. What are objective pronouns?

   i. What kind of pronoun do you use following a preposition?

   j. What is a reflexive pronoun?

   k. What do all reflexive pronouns end in?

   l. How are Biblical pronouns categorized?

   m. Name the demonstrative pronouns.

   n. What is an antecedent?

2. Have the students circle all the pronouns they can find from a newspaper or magazine article.

3. Have a student make his own Morse code. The student could take each letter of the alphabet and give it another symbol. After making a code he can let a friend decipher a message.

Section 3: Forming and Using Words

1. Discussion questions:

   a. Why is it necessary to know how to make new words out of basic or root words?

   b. Where are prefixes added to a word?

   c. Which prefix may change its spelling?

   d. When do adjectives become adverbs?

   e. What happens to a silent *e* following a consonant when the suffix *-ly* is added?

   f. When do adjectives become nouns?

   g. What do we call words that have the same sounds?

   h. How are proper nouns always written?

   i. Is it possible to add two suffixes to a word?

   j. Name two of the most common suffixes.

2. Write common words on the board and have the students tell you their homonyms.

3. Give a student a list of words and have him give the antonyms and synonyms for the words.

Administer the LIFEPAC Spelling Test.
The test is provided in this Teacher's Guide.
Evaluate the tests and review the words the students spelled incorrectly.
If necessary, review all of the words in the unit to prepare for the alternate spelling test.
Administer the Alternate LIFEPAC Spelling test that is provided in this Teacher's Guide.

Administer the LIFEPAC Test.
The test is to be administered in one session. Give no help except with directions.
Evaluate the tests and review areas where the students have done poorly.
Review the pages and activities that stress the concepts tested.
If necessary, administer the Alternate LIFEPAC Test.

ANSWER KEYS

SECTION 1

1.1   Hint:
Include books, notebooks, folders, pens, pencils, paper, and rulers.

1.2   Pictures will vary.

1.3   Examples:
a. lad
b. lass
c. couch, davenport
d. automobile
e. earth, soil
f. buddy
g. glance, see
h. infant
i. board
j. stream, rivulet

1.4   Pictures will vary.

1.5   Teacher check

1.6   Teacher check

1.7   Example:
Category: books
member: language arts
dictionary
mathematics

1.8   Example:
Category: organizers
member: paper clips
notebook
folder

1.9   Example:
Category: paper
member: construction
notebook
graph

1.10   Example:
Category: art supplies
member: crayons
pencils
paints

1.11-1.15

		Common label
1.11	~~Xerox~~	makes of cars
1.12	~~clouds~~	growing plants
1.13	~~lions~~	domestic (tame) animals
1.14	~~bacon~~	things with shells
1.15	~~Moses~~	some of the disciples

1.16   Any order:
a. Richard
b. Chicago
c. Arizona
d. Bible
e. Harvard
f. Mary
g. France
h. Mississippi River
i. David
j. Atlantic Ocean

1.17   Hint:
Be sure to capitalize the proper nouns.

1.18   a. cities
b. oceans
c. continents
d. Presidents of the United States

1.19-1.22 Hint:
Your librarian, Sunday school teacher, parents, or other adults in your town should be able to help you find this information. There are special books about the meanings of names.
— Parent check

1.23   Teacher check

1.24   a. ie
b. ei
c. ie
d. ie
e. ei
f. ei
g. ei
h. ei

1.25   a. audience
b. achieve
c. relief
d. siege
e. relieve
f. believe

1.26   a. leisure
b. receive
c. conceive
d. ceiling
e. neighbor
f. weigh

1.27 Sentences will vary.
Examples:

–To *achieve* means to accomplish something.

–An *antonym* is a word that means the opposite of another word.

–An *audience* is a group of people gathered in a place to see or hear.

–To *believe* is to accept something as real or true.

–A *category* is a group or division in a general system of classification.

–The *ceiling* is the inside, top covering of a room.

–*Communication* is the giving or exchanging of information or news.

–To *conceive* is to form an idea in the mind.

–*Dialect* is a variation of language spoken by a specific group of people.

–A *duplicate* is something exactly like something else.

–An *encyclopedia* is a book or set of books giving information on all branches of knowledge.

–*Harmony* is agreement of feelings, ideas, or actions.

–A *homonym* is a word having the same pronunciation, spelling, or both as another word.

–An *individual* is one person, animal, or thing.

–*Language* is human speech.

–*Leisure* is time free from required work in which a person may amuse himself.

–*Melody* is made up of musical sounds in agreeable succession or arrangement.

–*Neighbors* are people who live near other people.

–An *orchestra* is a group of musicians playing together on various instruments.

–To *originate* is to invent or cause to be.

–*Performance* is carrying out, or doing, a deed.

–To *receive* is to take into one's own hands or possession.

–*Relief* is the removal or lessening of some cause of pain or distress.

–To *relieve* means to set free from an obligation.

–A *siege* is the surrounding of a fortified place by enemy forces.

–A *synonym* is a word having the same or nearly the same meaning as another word.

–To *weigh* is to find the weight of something.

— Teacher check

SELF TEST 1

1.01   synonyms
1.02   dialects
1.03   noun
1.04   category
1.05   proper noun
1.06   making the workmen speak different languages
1.07   use the same labels for the same objects
1.08   Words represent objects and convey the idea of the object to the hearer.
1.09   cow
1.010 pets (household)
1.011 Genesis
1.012 books of the New Testament
1.013 sled
1.014 vehicles with wheels
1.015 ball
1.016 birds
1.017 pillow
1.018 musical instruments
1.019-1.033
Three categories; any order:
— States
— Planets
— Presidents
Four members; any order under specific category:
1.019 Category: States
1.020 Virginia
1.021 California
1.022 Wisconsin
1.023 Florida
1.024 Category: Planets
1.025 Mars
1.026 Earth
1.027 Neptune
1.028 Jupiter
1.029 Category: Presidents
1.030 Kennedy
1.031 Jefferson
1.032 Lincoln
1.033 Ford
1.034 specific
1.035 capitalize
1.036 Any order:
a.   descriptions
b.   famous events
c.   original settlers
d.   heroes
1.037 family occupations or locations

1.038-1.047 Any order:
1.038 Elizabeth
1.039 Egypt
1.040 Moses
1.041 America
1.042 Bible
1.043 Lake Erie
1.044 Kansas
1.045 Jonathan
1.046 New York
1.047 Europe

SECTION 2

2.1 Example:
On <u>my</u> tenth birthday <u>my</u> family gave <u>me</u> a puppy. Because <u>she</u> was red <u>we</u> called <u>her</u> Ginger. Ginger is like one of the family. <u>She</u> has <u>her</u> own bed in <u>my</u> room and <u>her</u> own dish in the kitchen. <u>I</u> even gave <u>her</u> a blanket and some toys. <u>She</u> can sit and beg. <u>She</u> likes to be tickled and brushed. <u>I</u> take <u>her</u> for a walk every day.

2.2 Example:
On Billy James' tenth birthday Billy James' family gave Billy James a puppy. Because the puppy was red Billy James' family called the puppy Ginger. Ginger is just like one of the family. Ginger has Ginger's own bed in Billy James' room and Ginger's own dish in the kitchen. Billy James even gave Ginger a blanket and some toys. Ginger can sit and beg. Ginger likes to be tickled and brushed. Billy James takes Ginger for a walk every day.

2.3 Teacher check

2.4
a. her
b. her
c. They
d. her
e. she
f. them
g. you
h. I
i. Your
j. my
k. Your
l. my

2.5 turned back on itself

2.6 The action in the sentence is turned back on the actor (subject) when one is used.

2.7 myself, ourselves, yourself, yourselves, himself, herself, itself, themselves

2.8 Sentences will vary.
Check for subject/reflexive pronoun agreement.

2.9

Nominative	Objective	Possessive
a. I	a. me	a. my
b. He	b. me	b. my
c. he	c. me	c. his
d. He	d. me	d. thy
e. he	e. me	e. thy
f. I	f. me	f. mine
g. I	g. me	g. my
h. thou		h. my
i. they		i. my
j. Thou		
k. thou		
l. I		

2.10   <u>S</u>
      this   these
      that   those
2.11 that – those
2.12 this – these
2.13 Teacher check
2.14 Circle she.   Draw arrow to Sally.
2.15 Circle his.   Draw arrow to Jeff.
      Circle They.   Draw arrow to flowers.
2.16 Circle her.   Draw arrow to Carole.
2.17 Circle their.   Draw arrows to Lisa; Beth.
2.18 his
2.19 their
2.20 me
2.21 themselves
2.22 he
2.23 Sentences will vary.
      Examples:
      a. An *anecdote* is a short account of some
          interesting incident or event.
      b. An *antecedent* is the noun referred to by
          a pronoun.
      c. An *antidote* refers to medicine or a
          remedy.
      d. An *apostrophe* is a mark used to show the
          omission of letters in contractions.
      e. *Comprehension* is the act or power of
          understanding.
      f. A *demonstrative* word points out an
          object.
      g. To be *disrespectful* is to show no courtesy.
      h. *Increase* is to make greater or more
          numerous.
      i. *Nominative* refers to a pronoun case
          used as the subject or the predicate
          nominative of a verb.
      j. *Objective* refers to a pronoun case used
          as the direct object of a verb or as the
          object of a preposition.
      k. *Possessive* refers to the case of pronouns
          showing ownership.
      l. A *prefix* is a word or a syllable used at
          the beginning of a word to change its
          meaning or to form another word.
      m. *Reflexive* refers to pronouns ending in self
          or selves referring back to the subject.
      n. A *suffix* in an addition made at the end
          of a word to form another word of a
          different meaning or function.
      o. Someone *undistinguished* is not famous
          or well known.
      p. *Uninterrupted* means continuous.
      — Teacher check

2.24 Sentences will vary.
      Be sure homonyms are used correctly and
      sentences are punctuated correctly.
      Examples:
      a. The golf course has coarse grass.
      b. Did you see the dear little deer?
      c. The coal has been in the bin.
      d. Come here and hear this noise.

34

SELF TEST 2

2.01	the Tower of Babel		**2.034**	Any order:
2.02	code			a. that
2.03	synonyms			b. these
2.04	dialects			c. this
2.05	related			d. those
2.06	red (answers will vary)		**2.035**	this
2.07	a. capitalized		**2.036**	that
	b. specific		**2.037**	near
2.08	noun		**2.038**	farther away
2.09	personal		**2.039**	adjectives
2.010	demonstrative		**2.040**	people
2.011	ownership		**2.041**	Thou
2.012	a. self		**2.042**	Thee
	b. selves		**2.043-2.045** Either order:	
2.013	nominative		**2.043**	Thy
2.014	objective		**2.044**	Thine
2.015	Any order:		**2.045**	Thyself

2.046

Nouns	Pronouns
Jerry	their
Tim	They
books	it
library	his
Tim	She
book	it
librarian	himself
cart	they
Jerry	
corner	
cart	
library	

2.015 Any order:
- a. my
- b. mine
- c. our
- d. ours
- e. your
- f. yours
- g. his
- h. her
- I. hers
- j. its
- k. their
- l. theirs

2.016 his
2.017 our
2.018 their
2.019 her
2.020 your
2.021 My
2.022 its
2.023 mine
2.024-2.033 <u>Reflexive pronoun</u>
2.024 _C_ itself
2.025 _I_ myself
2.026 _C_ himself
2.027 _C_ yourself
2.028 _C_ myself
2.029 _C_ ourselves
2.030 _me_ myself
2.031 _C_ themselves
2.032 _me_ myself
2.033 _C_ herself

SECTION 3

3.1 The prefixes change the meaning of the root word.

3.2 Sentences will vary.
  a. unattractive—
     The vase was unattractive.
  b. unchanged—
     Her condition remains unchanged.
  c. unwelcome—
     People who misbehave are unwelcome here.

3.3 Sentences will vary.
  a. premature—
     The baby was premature.
  b. precaution—
     Checking the gas, oil, and water in the car is a good precaution.
  c. prejudge—
     Do not prejudge before you have heard all the facts.

3.4 Sentences will vary.
  a. antifreeze—
     Use antifreeze in your car radiator.
  b. antisocial—
     His behavior was antisocial.
  c. antiseptic—
     Put antiseptic on that cut.

3.5 Sentences will vary.
  a. discomfort—
     The bone is broken, but he has little discomfort.
  b. discolor—
     The sun can discolor certain fabrics.
  c. disadvantage—
     He puts me to a great disadvantage.

3.6 illogical
3.7 irregular
3.8 immature
3.9 inappropriate
3.10 irretrievable
3.11 insufficient
3.12 impossible
3.13 immeasurable
3.14 illiterate
3.15 improbable
3.16 Nothing, it stays with the root.
3.17 It is changed to *i*.
3.18
  a. smoothly
  b. princely
  c. showily
  d. sincerely
  e. snappily

3.19
  a. happiness
  b. goodness
  c. funniness
  d. rudeness
  e. dimness
3.20 Examples:
  a. The horse swiftly won the race.
  b. Due to his swiftness, the horse won the race.
3.21 Examples:
  a. I completely read the book.
  b. Completion of the book was required by the teacher.
3.22 Examples:
  a. The child happily opened the gift.
  b. The child opened the gift in happiness.
3.23 Examples:
  a. The class that worked quietly was praised.
  b. The class was praised for its quietness.
3.24-3.43 Correct words:
3.24 altar
3.25 been
3.26 buy, by
3.27 break
3.28 capital
3.29 course
3.30 Council
3.31 dear
3.32 dessert
3.33 here, hear
3.34 led
3.35 passed
3.36 peace, piece
3.37 plains
3.38 principal
3.39 shown
3.40 stationary
3.41 they're, their, there
3.42 through
3.43 too, to, two
3.44

ACROSS	DOWN
1. principle	1. peace
3. past	2. led
5. desert	4. stationary
6. alter	7. there
8. council	9. lead
10. principal	12. shown
11. altar	13. through
12. stationery	15. piece
14. too	16. counsel
15. plane	17. their
17. threw	
18. dessert	
19. capitol	

SELF TEST 3

3.01	synonyms		**3.043**	stationary
3.02	category		**3.044**	Their
3.03	noun		**3.045**	principle
3.04	dialect		**3.046**	council
3.05	prefix		**3.047**	through
3.06	suffix		**3.048**	alter
3.07	homonyms		**3.049**	bin
3.08	pronoun		**3.050**	brake
3.09	demonstrative		**3.051**	by
3.010	possessive		**3.052**	capital
3.011-3.013 Examples:			**3.053**	coarse
3.011	scared		**3.054**	counsel
3.012	volume		**3.055**	desert
3.013	ship			
3.014	flowers			
3.015	Example: daisy			
3.016	pre			
3.017	anti			
3.018	in			
3.019	un			
3.020	il			
3.021	dis			
3.022	im			
3.023	anti			
3.024	ir			
3.025	dis			
3.026	im			
3.027	dis *or* un			
3.028	im			
3.029	un			
3.030	pre *or* in			
3.031	friendliness			
3.032	gamely			
3.033	lonesomeness			
3.034	merrily			
3.035	finally			
3.036	sadness			
3.037	handily			
3.038	shakiness			
3.039	finely			
3.040	suddenly			

3.041 Any order:
   a. nominative
   b. possessive
   c. objective

3.042 a. my/mine
   b. our/ours
   c. his
   d. your(s)
   e. its
   f. their(s)

LIFEPAC TEST

1. synonyms
2. homonyms
3. possessive pronouns
4. reflexive pronouns
5. demonstrative pronouns
6. proper nouns
7. prefixes
8. suffixes
9. antecedent
10. category
11. c
12. d
13. a
14. e
15. b
16.-23. Three categories; any order:
    — colors
    — course subject
    — relatives
    Three members; any order under
    specific category:
16. Category: colors
17. red
18. blue
19. orange
20. Category: course subject
21. English
22. math
23. science
24. Category: relatives
25. brother
26. niece
27. aunt
28.-32. Examples:
28. First Bible Church
29. Lake Superior
30. Hudson River
31. Bible
32. San Francisco
33. antifreeze
34. predestination
35. illiterate
36. uncomfortable
37. disagree
38. angrily
39. dirtiness
40. homely
41. gladness
42. openness

43. a. *i*   b. *e*
44. *c*
45. *a*
46. releive
47. shone
48. dessert
49. Capitol
50. stationery
51. too
52. This
53. That
54. Those
55. These
56. nouns
57. his
58. my
59. our
60. their
61. your
62. ourselves
63. himself
64. yourself *or* yourselves
65. themselves
66. itself
67. Answer should include:
    creation of languages;
    confusion of labels;
    disruption of communication
68. Answer should include:
    variations within languages;
    different labels for same objects

ALTERNATE LIFEPAC TEST

1. synonyms
2. proper nouns
3. common nouns
4. personal pronouns
5. reflexive pronouns
6. demonstrative pronouns
7. prefixes
8. suffixes
9. antecedent
10. category
11. f
12. a
13. e
14. c
15. b
16.-27. Three categories; any order:
— proper name
— fruit
— flowers
Three members; any order under specific category:
16. Category: proper name
17. Jones
18. James
19. Matthew
20. Category: fruit
21. pear
22. lemon
23. apple
24. Category: flowers
25. rose
26. daisy
27. petunia
28. Example:
Ford
29. Example:
Black Beauty
30. Example:
Heritage
31. Example:
Chicago
32. Example:
Arizona
33. discolor
34. prearrange
35. inconsiderate
36. unchanged
37. disobey

38. happily
39. hardness
40. friendly
41. kindness
42. heaviness
43. a. *i*
b. *e*
44. liesure
45. been
46. buy
47. course
48. here
49. passed
50. noun
51. inanimate *or* nonliving
52. these
53. that
54. close
55. Examples:
mine, hers, his, yours
56. Example:
their
57. Examples:
his, her, my, their, our, your
58. his
59. us
60. himself
61. yourself
62. themselves
63. himself
64. yourself
65. Example:
Some places are named because of geographic features (Long Island).
Others were named for important events, heroes, and founding groups.
Personal names often reflected what the person did for a living (miller/Miller).
Others represented a quality (Amy: *Beloved*— Earl: *Noble*).
66. Example:
Each word is a symbol or label that represents an object or idea.
Some objects have more than one label and these duplicate labels are called synonyms.
Dialects also cause duplication.

SPELLING TEST

1	originate	Did that idea **originate** with you?	originate
2	antonym	The **antonym** of large is small.	antonym
3	believe	I **believe** you are telling the truth.	believe
4	encyclopedia	Use the **encyclopedia** for your report.	encyclopedia
5	audience	The **audience** became quiet.	audience
6	individual	Try to resolve your **individual** differences.	individual
7	neighbor	Mrs. Smith is our closest **neighbor**.	neighbor
8	duplicate	It is a waste of time to **duplicate** efforts.	duplicate
9	language	What **language** do you speak?	language
10	ceiling	The **ceiling** needs painting.	ceiling
11	harmony	They sang in perfect **harmony**.	harmony
12	orchestra	The **orchestra** played selections by Bach.	orchestra
13	relief	His **relief** was apparent by his smile.	relief
14	receive	You should **receive** my letter soon.	receive
15	leisure	I read in my **leisure** time.	leisure
16	category	In which **category** does that tree belong?	category
17	communication	Language is a form of **communication**.	communication
18	antecedent	The pronoun must have an **antecedent**.	antecedent
19	bin	She poured the flour into the **bin**.	bin
20	prefix	Add a **prefix** to that word.	prefix
21	nominative	This noun is a predicate **nominative**.	nominative
22	possessive	His is the **possessive** form of he.	possessive
23	apostrophe	Use an **apostrophe** "s" to show possession.	apostrophe
24	coarse	The cloth is very thick and **coarse**.	coarse
25	here	"I am right **here**," his father said.	here

SPELLING TEST

26	uninterrupted	I want **uninterrupted** silence.	uninterrupted
27	course	The **course** of the river has changed.	course
28	comprehension	Read for **comprehension** and enjoyment.	comprehension
29	antidote	The doctor gave the **antidote** for the poison.	antidote
30	increase	As you grow older you will **increase** in size.	increase
31	disrespectful	Do not speak in a **disrespectful** way.	disrespectful
32	anecdote	Uncle Andy told a funny **anecdote**.	anecdote
33	suffix	Add a **suffix** at the end of the word.	suffix
34	there	Your book is over **there**.	there
35	peace	We hope for **peace** on Earth.	peace
36	stationery	Tammy used her **stationery** to write a letter.	stationery
37	desert	It is hot and dry in the **desert**.	desert
38	past	It was **past** noon when it happened.	past
39	alter	We must **alter** our plans.	alter
40	principal	Our **principal** is a good administrator.	principal
41	they're	Do not call the youngest children; **they're** asleep already.	they're
42	council	He is a member of the student **council**.	council
43	piece	Do you want a **piece** of cake?	piece
44	dessert	I want pie for **dessert**.	dessert
45	stationary	The parked car is **stationary**.	stationary
46	counsel	The minister gave them **counsel** last week.	counsel
47	their	They picked up **their** books.	their
48	altar	The Bible was on the **altar** at the church.	altar
49	principle	Do you understand the **principle** of gravity?	principle

LANGUAGE ARTS 701

ALTERNATE LIFEPAC TEST

NAME _____

DATE _____

SCORE _____

90
113

Complete these sentences (each answer, 2 points).

1. Two words having the same meaning are called _____ .

2. *Arizona* and *Indiana* are classified as _____ _____ .

3. *Girl* and *boy* are classified as _____ _____ .

4. *You* and *me* are classified as _____ _____ .

5. *Myself* and *yourselves* are called _____ _____ .

6. *These* and *those* are considered _____ _____ .

7. *Un-* and *anti-* are called _____ .

8. A term for *-ly* and *-ness* is _____ .

9. The noun to which a pronoun refers is called a(an) _____ .

10. A group of related objects belong to the same _____ .

Match these synonyms (each answer, 2 points).

11. _____ baby   a. joyful

12. _____ glad   b. home

13. _____ fast   c. say

14. _____ tell   d. go

15. _____ house   e. swift

                             f. infant

Sort the following list of words into three categories. Write the name of the category in the first blank provided. Write the members of this category on the remaining three lines (each category name, 2 points; each member item, 1 point).

pear	rose	apple
Jones	lemon	Matthew
John	daisy	petunia

16. Category: _____

17. _____

18. _____

19. _____

20. Category: _____

21. _____

22. _____

23. _____

24. Category: _____

25. _____

26. _____

27. _____

Write a proper noun for each common noun (each answer, 1 point).

28. car _____

29. book _____

30. school _____

31. city _____

32. state _____

Write the correct word. Watch for spelling changes (each answer, 1 point).

33. *dis* + color _____

34. *pre* + arrange _____

35. *in* + considerate _____

36. *un* + changed _____

37. *dis* + obey _____

Write the correct word. Watch for spelling changes (each answer, 1 point).

38. happy + *ly* _____

39. hard + *ness* _____

40. friend + *ly* _____

41. kind + *ness* _____

42. heavy + *ness* _____

Complete the following jingle (each answer, 1 point).

43. a. _____ before b. _____ , except after *c*.

Circle the misspelled word (this answer, 1 point).

44. receive   relieve   liesure   believe

Circle the correct word (each answer, 2 points).

45. Where have you (been / bin)?

46. I want to (buy / by) that book.

47. The Red Cross offers a (coarse / course) in first aid.

48. Let's sit (here / hear).

49. We have already (passed / past) Mary's house.

Complete these statements with the appropriate demonstrative pronouns (each answer, 2 points).

50. *This*, *that*, *these*, and *those* function as adjectives if they modify a(n) _____ .

51. Demonstrative pronouns indicate _____ objects .

52. The plural of *this* is _____ .

53. The singular of *those* is _____ .

54. *This* and *these* indicate that the object or objects are _____ to the speaker.

Complete these statements with the appropriate possessive pronouns (each answer, 2 points).

55. That bike is _____ .

56. The children sang _____ song.

57. This is _____ room.

58. The boy lost _____ book.

59. John and I bought that book; it belongs to _____ .

Complete these statements with the appropriate reflexive pronouns (each answer, 2 points).

60. John wrote the letter all by _____ .

61. I want you to make your bed all by _____ .

62. Let them do it by _____ .

63. John hurt _____ .

64. Speak for _____ .

Answer these questions using complete sentences (each answer, 5 points).

65. How are some places named and what are the meanings of some personal names?

_____

_____

_____

_____

_____

_____

66. Why is all language a code?

_____

_____

_____

_____

_____

_____

ALTERNATE SPELLING TEST

1	originate	Does the Nile **originate** in Egypt?	originate
2	antonym	An **antonym** is a word having an opposite meaning.	antonym
3	believe	Do you **believe** his story?	believe
4	encyclopedia	I cannot find the "M" volume of the **encyclopedia**.	encyclopedia
5	audience	The **audience** applauded the performance.	audience
6	individual	Serve the cake on **individual** plates.	individual
7	neighbor	My **neighbor** has a new dog.	neighbor
8	duplicate	Send the **duplicate** and keep the original.	duplicate
9	harmony	Your use of colors should produce **harmony**.	harmony
10	language	I want to learn a foreign **language**.	language
11	ceiling	There is a fly on the **ceiling** in the living room.	ceiling
12	orchestra	Have you heard our city **orchestra** play?	orchestra
13	relief	The rain was a welcome **relief** from the dry weather.	relief
14	receive	Will he **receive** a Christmas card from them?	receive
15	leisure	Hobbies are enjoyable **leisure** activities.	leisure
16	category	Does the word "basketball" fit that **category**?	category
17	communication	Sign language is used for **communication**.	communication
18	antecedent	The **antecedent** of "his" is John.	antecedent
19	bin	The vegetable **bin** is full.	bin
20	prefix	"Anti-" is a **prefix** in our spelling list.	prefix
21	nominative	The **nominative** case is used for subjects.	nominative
22	possessive	She is a **possessive** mother.	possessive
23	hear	What do I **hear**?	hear
24	been	I have **been** sick for two days.	been
25	plain	Use **plain** common sense to solve the problem.	plain

ALTERNATE SPELLING TEST

26	apostrophe	An **apostrophe** is needed in contractions.	apostrophe
27	coarse	**Coarse** sand can hurt your feet.	coarse
28	here	**Here** is your hat.	here
29	uninterrupted	The game was **uninterrupted**.	uninterrupted
30	dialect	Which **dialect** does he speak?	dialect
31	synonym	"Big" is a **synonym** for large.	synonym
32	melody	They played a simple **melody** on the piano.	melody
33	weigh	Did they **weigh** you yesterday?	weigh
34	relieve	That man will **relieve** the guard at noon.	relieve
35	conceive	He did **conceive** that idea.	conceive
36	siege	Many people died in the **siege** of Vicksburg.	siege
37	homonym	"Hare" is a **homonym** of hair.	homonym
38	achieve	Did you **achieve** much in school today?	achieve
39	performance	The orchestra gave a tremendous **performance**.	performance
40	lead	**Lead** shields are used in x-ray rooms.	lead
41	led	Alice **led** the boys to the right room.	led
42	passed	I **passed** to the seventh grade.	passed
43	plane	By **plane** it's only a three hour trip.	plane
44	threw	Valerie **threw** the ball to Joey.	threw
45	through	Brad walked **through** the door.	through
46	reflexive	"Himself" is a **reflexive** pronoun.	reflexive
47	objective	The **objective** case of "he" is him.	objective
48	demonstrative	A **demonstrative** pronoun points out an object.	demonstrative
49	deer	A baby **deer** is a fawn.	deer
50	stationary	That post is **stationary**.	stationary

LANGUAGE ARTS 702

Unit 2: More Word Usage

TEACHER NOTES

MATERIALS NEEDED FOR LIFEPAC	
Required	Suggested
None	• King James Version of the Bible • dictionary • reference books or online sources

ADDITIONAL LEARNING ACTIVITIES

Section 1: Speaking Expressively

1. Discussion questions:

   a. Is listening an active skill? Why or why not?

   b. What is more easily understood, speech or written words? Why or why not?

   c. What unique gift did God give man?

   d. What determines the message people receive from us?

   e. What helps us interpret the feelings of other people more accurately?

   f. What is reflected by tone of voice?

   g. What are some of the tones we should avoid?

   h. What are some tones that convey Christian love?

   i. What controls the pitch of our voice?

   j. What are junctures?

   k. How do syllables affect our speech?

   l. What are some ways we can express meaning when we read orally?

   m. What are some things you must remember when telling a story?

   n. Why is it important to understand the characters of a story before telling the story?

2. Choose a Psalm and divide a group of students into high and low voices. Have the students memorize the Psalm and give it as a choral reading.

3. Have a student choose and read a poem to the class with expression and feeling?

Section 2: Listening Attentively

1. Discussion questions:

   a. Why is it important to listen carefully?

   b. What kind of listening takes place when a person listens to background music?

    c. What kind of listening do we do when announcements are being made?

    d. Name three listening hints.

    e. What kind of listening do we do when we compare information with what we already know?

    f. What are some hints to help us decide whether we should believe what we hear?

    g. When do we use appreciative listening?

    h. What is propaganda?

2. Have the students memorize the Preamble to the Constitution of the United States of America and give it as a choral reading.

3. Have a student choose a Psalm or a chapter from Proverbs and read it to the class. Have the student use the required expressions and feelings.

Section 3: Using Verbs Correctly

1. Discussion questions:

    a. Why is it important to know the structure or building blocks of speech?

    b. What are probably the most important words in a sentence?

    c. What is an auxiliary verb?

    d. What is a verb?

    e. What is a predicate verb?

    f. What are verb inflections?

    g. Where does a verb usually appear in a sentence?

    h. What do we mean by verb tense?

    i. What are two classifications of verbs?

    j. When do we use present tense verbs?

    k. Which tense remains the same for all persons, singular or plural?

    l. When do we use the word *shall*?

    m. What do we mean by conjugating a verb?

    n. What are the three principal parts of a verb?

    o. Name the six tenses of verbs.

2. Have some students pretend they are calling their children to supper using different intonations. Have the other students identify the feelings expressed.

3. Have a student close his eyes and record the different sounds that he hears happening around the class. This activity is a good listening drill.

Administer the LIFEPAC Spelling Test.

The test is provided in this Teacher's Guide.

Evaluate the tests and review the words the students spelled incorrectly.

If necessary, review all of the words in the unit to prepare for the alternate spelling test.

Administer the Alternate LIFEPAC Spelling test that is provided in this Teacher's Guide.

Administer the LIFEPAC Test.

The test is to be administered in one session. Give no help except with directions.

Evaluate the tests and review areas where the students have done poorly.

Review the pages and activities that stress the concepts tested.

If necessary, administer the Alternate LIFEPAC Test.

ANSWER KEYS

SECTION 1

1.1 Teacher check
1.2 Word
1.3 God
1.4 intonations
1.5 tone
1.6 pitches
1.7 Either order:
a. length
b. thickness
1.8 larynx
1.9 changed
1.10 pleasant
or cheerful
1.11 juncture
1.12 3 bar
2 em
1 go
1.13 3 to
2 Oc
1 ber
1.14 3 sour
2 Mis
1 i
1.15 3 ta
2 po
1 to
1.16 3 grat
2 i
1 fy
1.17 3 gard
2 dis
1 re
1.18 3 spect
2 dis
1 re
1.19 3 clar
2 i
1 fy
1.20 3 a
2 cre
1 tion
1.21 3 a
2 pri
1 cot

1.22 wrist
dia
a mond watch
1.23 birth
a day par
ty
1.24 bright
sunny
day
a
1.25 cem
last
the of De
ber
1.26 good
whole some
food
a
1.27 Teacher check
1.28 Teacher check
1.29 courteous courageous kind
just honest humble
forgiving
1.30 King Alfred admitted he was to blame.
1.31 hospitality, compassion, generosity, rudeness, anger, forgiveness, gratefulness
1.32 He may have been a hard worker.
He showed respect for those in authority.
1.33 He was ashamed.
1.34 He bowed his head.
1.35 Hint:
Include feelings of shame and embarrassment.
1.36 She was gripped with fear.
She was humiliated and asked for forgiveness.
1.37 forgiving and being forgiven
1.38 Examples:
The woodcutter's wife recovered from her temporary anger.
She lost her anger and became reasonable and kind.
She felt relief.
She was grateful.
1.39 God
or Jesus
1.40 no

1.41 She could have forgiven the stranger at once and aired the house out, reassuring him that anyone could make a mistake. Then graciously she could have baked more cakes.

1.42 Examples:
poor ragged shepherd; old hut with smoke pouring out of the chimney; immersed in his thoughts; oblivious to the rising smoke; fear gripped the heart; poured over her like warm summer rain.

1.43 Teacher check

1.44 Alphabetize and define each word of Spelling Words-1 using complete sentences.
Sentences will vary.
Examples:

antagonism –
  Antagonism means hostility.

appreciate –
  To *appreciate* means to value highly.

appropriate –
  To be *appropriate* means to be especially right or proper.

convey –
  To *convey* an idea means to express it.

designate –
  To *designate* means to point out.

embarrassed –
  To be *embarrassed* means to be disturbed or confused.

enunciate –
  To *enunciate* means to speak or pronounce words distinctly.

erroneous –
  Something *erroneous* is mistaken or incorrect.

evaluate –
  To *evaluate* is to judge.

fortunate –
  To be *fortunate* means having good success.

imitate –
  To *imitate* is to try to be like someone else.

impatience –
  Impatience is unwillingness to put up with delay.

inattention –
  Inattention is carelessness.

interpret –
  To *interpret* means to explain the meaning of something.

juncture –
  Juncture is a pause between sounds, words, or phrases.

logical –
  Something *logical* is reasonably expected.

oblivious –
  Oblivious means not mindful.

persuaded –
  Persuaded is to be won over.

persuasion –
  Persuasion means winning another person over to your idea or belief.

precise –
  Precise means to be exact, accurate, and definite.

premise –
  A *premise* is a statement assumed to be true and used to draw a conclusion.

previous –
  Previous refers to something coming before.

propaganda –
  Propaganda is a plan for spreading beliefs or opinions.

relationship –
  A *relationship* is a condition of belonging to the same family.

resurrection –
  Resurrection is a coming to life again.

structure –
  A *structure* is something built.

temporary –
  Something *temporary* is not permanent.

— Teacher check

SELF TEST 1

1.01 Example:
To choose the correct word to convey the exact meaning; to cultivate a pleasant cheerful tone; to avoid hurting others.

1.02 *Stress* is force or emphasis placed on a spoken word or part of a word.

1.03 *Pitch* is the rise and fall of the voice.

1.04 *Juncture* is pause in word phrase or sentence for clarity or emphasis.

1.05 the Word

1.06 tone of voice

1.07 character traits

1.08 Examples:
a. anger
b. impatience
c. fear

1.09 larynx

1.010 true

1.011 false

1.012 false

1.013 true

1.014 false

1.015 true

1.016 true

1.017 3 al
2 pha
1 bet

1.018 3 gan
2 prop
1 a da

1.019 3 tro
2 con
1 ling

1.020 3 lim
2 nate
1 e i

1.021 a. Choose a story you enjoy.
b. Know the story and the order of its events.
c. Understand the character traits of the people involved.
d. Use colorful words and expressions to reveal feelings and attitudes or for special effect.
e. Pause whenever necessary to emphasize a word or phrase.
f. Use pitch and stress to lend variety and meaning to your voice.

SECTION 2

2.1 Examples:
A book drops.
A chair squeaks.

2.2 Examples:
A car passes.
A dog barks.

2.3 Examples:
someone whispering
footsteps
clock ticking

2.4 No. A person must listen more carefully.

2.5 a. noise
b. lands
c. gladness
d. presence
e. the Lord
f. made us
g. ourselves
h. sheep
i. gates
j. praise
k. His name
l. good
m. truth

2.6 Teacher check

2.7 Examples:
He didn't like the teams playing.
He has a test to study for.

2.8 a. Example:
How To Make An Omelet
b. Examples:
breaking an egg, chopping vegetables, heating butter, pans needed
c. Example:
scrambling eggs

2.9 Teacher check

2.10 _3_ Your best friend tells you that potatoes are more nutritious than bread.
_4_ A new friend says that shoplifting does not really hurt anybody.
_2_ Betty, who is angry with Ted, says she hates boys.
_1_ A politician says all taxes are unfair.
_1_ A reporter says accidents are caused by weather changes.

2.11 Teacher check

2.12 Alphabetize and use each word of Spelling Words-2 in a sentence, demonstrating the meaning of each word.

Sentences will vary.

Examples:

abridgment –
   That copy is an *abridgment* of the original.

academy –
   Will you attend the *academy* next year?

accompaniment –
   He sang without *accompaniment*.

bankruptcy –
   Ike filed for *bankruptcy* after his business failed.

bazaar –
   The school *bazaar* will be next week.

becoming –
   He is *becoming* a skillful swimmer.

catalogue –
   You might find a picture of that shirt in a *catalogue*.

desperate –
   His check is late, so he is becoming *desperate*.

emphasize –
   You need to *emphasize* the sound.

foreigner –
   You would be a *foreigner* in New Zealand.

granddaughter –
   Mrs. White's *granddaughter* is here.

humorous –
   I heard a *humorous* story today.

icing –
   Please spread the *icing* on the cake.

judgment –
   Use your own *judgment*.

knowledge –
   Knowledge can lead to wisdom.

lying –
   The cat was *lying* on the chair.

mayonnaise –
   Do you use *mayonnaise* or mustard?

nickel –
   The machine takes dimes and *nickels*.

omelet –
   A western *omelet* is delicious.

parallel –
   Are those lines *parallel*?

quite –
   I am not *quite* finished.

really –
   Are you *really* coming?

sandwich –
   Have a *sandwich*.

technical –
   Some *technical* words have been invented as a result of the space age.

until –
   I may stay *until* mother calls.

villain –
   George played the hero's part, and Tim was the *villain*.

woolly –
   The sheep was very *woolly*.

yacht –
   His *yacht* sails for South America tomorrow.

zoology –
   Have you studied your *zoology*?

— Teacher check

SELF TEST 2

2.01 stress
2.02 pitch
2.03 juncture
2.04 intonations
2.05 feelings
or thoughts
2.06 larynx
2.07 passive listening
2.08 purposeful
2.09 appreciative
2.010 critical
2.011 a. Choose a story you like.
     b. Know the story.
     c. Understand the characters involved.
     d. Use colorful words and expressions.
     e. Pause whenever necessary for effect.
     f. Use pitch and stress.
2.012 Any six of these:
     a. Be comfortable, but not too comfortable.
     b. Listen for key words or phrases.
     c. Watch for speaker clues; pauses,
        gestures, about important information.
     d. Listen for the speaker to sum up his talk.
     e. Be sure to take notes on key information.
     f. Ask questions whenever possible.
     or Compare the new information with what
        you already know.
2.013 a. Do I know the statement is based on fact?
     b. Is fact colored or affected by emotion?
     c. Do I want to believe this simply because it
        was stated by someone I like or admire?
     d. Does this statement agree with those
        Christian ideas and standards I have been
        taught?
2.014 3   gard
       2 dis
       1   re
2.015 3 el
       2   e
       1   phant

SECTION 3

3.1-3.10
    Third person singular s
3.1 arrives
3.2 finishes
3.3 waits
3.4 changes
3.5 studies
3.6 chases
3.7 mixes
3.8 carries
3.9 washes
3.10 prays
3.11-3.20
    Past tense
3.11 arrived
3.12 finished
3.13 waited
3.14 changed
3.15 studied
3.16 chased
3.17 mixed
3.18 carried
3.19 washed
3.20 prayed
3.21-3.30

	Past	Past participle
3.21	wrote	written
3.22	took	taken
3.23	raised	raised
3.24	got	got / gotten
3.25	dragged	dragged
3.26	sprang / spring	sprung
3.27	shrank / shrunk /	shrunken
3.28	led	led
3.29	dived / dove	dived
3.30	bore	borne / born

3.31 am / was
3.32 is / was
3.33 are / were
3.34 were
3.35 is / was
3.36 is / was
3.37 are / were
3.38 were
3.39 are / were
3.40 were
3.41 has
3.42 did
3.43 have
3.44 Does
3.45 did

3.46-3.55

	Verb stem	Future tense
3.46	arrive	shall / will
3.47	finish	shall / will
3.48	wait	shall / will
3.49	change	shall / will
3.50	study	shall / will
3.51	chase	shall / will
3.52	mix	shall / will
3.53	carry	shall / will
3.54	wash	shall / will
3.55	pray	shall / will
3.56	have	drunk
3.57	has	made
3.58	have	given
3.59	has	ridden
3.60	have	spoken

3.61-3.65 Hint:
- Check to see that the present perfect tense is used.
- See that the action began in the past but describes a present situation.
- Auxiliary verbs are *have* or *has* in third person singular.
- Be sure capitalization and punctuation are included correctly.

3.66	had	asked
3.67	had	forgotten
3.68	had	swum
3.69	had	flown
3.70	had	grown
3.71	had	spoken

3.72-3.76 Hint:
- Be sure the action expressed is past action completed before another past action.
- Auxiliary verb is *had*.
- Check capitalization and end punctuation.

3.77	(I) shall / will have built
3.78	(I) shall / will have blown
3.79	(I) shall / will have frozen
3.80	(I) shall / will have driven
3.81	(He) shall / will have climbed

3.82 Hint:
- Be sure the action expressed is completed before a set future time.
- Auxiliary verbs are *shall have* and *will have*.
- Check capitalization and end punctuation.

3.83
a. he / she / it grows
b. he / she / it grew
c. he / she / it will grow
d. he / she / it has grown
e. he / she / it had grown
f. he / she / it will have grown

3.84 Alphabetize the preceding words and write the definition of each one.
Sentences will vary.
Examples:

anonymous	–	having no name
argument	–	discussion by persons who disagree
athlete	–	a person trained to do physical exercises
balance	–	equality in weight
candidate	–	a person seeking office or honor
compel	–	drive or urge with force
courteous	–	thoughtful of others, polite
definite	–	clear or exact
disastrous	–	causing much suffering or loss
earnest	–	strong and firm in purpose
finally	–	at the end, at last
grammar	–	scientific study of forms, uses, and sounds of words in a language
height	–	measurement from top to bottom
infinite	–	without limits or bounds
lose	–	not having any longer
muscle	–	body cell consisting of contracting fibers
nowadays	–	at the present day
original	–	the first or earliest
presence	–	condition of being in a place
procedure	–	method of doing things
pursue	–	to strive for; try to get
recommend	–	to speak in favor of
similar	–	much the same
since	–	from a past time continuously till now
studying	–	an effort to learn by reading or thinking
temperament	–	a person's nature or disposition
weather	–	the condition of the atmosphere with respect to temperature, moisture, wind
whether	–	expresses a choice

— Teacher check

SELF TEST 3

3.01 Christian love

3.02 Any order:
a. stress
b. pitch
c. juncture

3.03 Example:
background music while reading

3.04 Examples:
directions
announcements
important information

3.05 Example:
political speeches

3.06 Example:
listen to a concert or play

3.07 a verb

3.08 an auxiliary verb

3.09 Any order:
a. regular
b. irregular

3.010 time

3.011 inflections

3.012 Any order:
a. present
b. past
c. past participle

3.013 Any order:
a. present
b. past
c. future
d. present perfect
e. past perfect
f. future perfect

3.014 Examples:
a. be
b. swim
c. shake

3.015 through words, tone of voice, gestures, and intonation

3.016 give information, give comfort, bring truth, Christian influence, or cause hurt

3.017 propaganda – a plan or method for spreading opinions or beliefs
Examples:
political speeches
commercials

3.018-3.026 Examples:

3.018 Had

3.019 will have bought

3.020 came

3.021 am

3.022 has jogged

3.023 will go

3.024 has taught

3.025 a. have finished
b. will go

3.026 had been spotted

LIFEPAC TEST

1. Either order:
   a. good (comfort)
   b. evil (hurt, harm)
2. Any order:
   a. stress
   b. pitch
   c. juncture
3. Either order:
   a. feelings and emotions
   b. thoughts
4. Any order:
   a. passive
   b. purposeful
   c. critical
   d. appreciative
5. propaganda
6. attitudes and character traits
7. be
8. e
9. i
10. a
11. f
12. g
13. c
14. h
15. j
16. b
17. d
18. Choose from:
    a. Be comfortable.
    b. Listen for key words.
    c. Watch for speaker clues.
    d. Listen for summary.
    or Note key information.
    Ask questions.
    Compare new information
    with old information.
19. Any order:
    a. present
    b. past
    c. future
    d. present perfect
    e. past perfect
    f. future perfect
20. When evaluating the truth of statements, political speeches, commercials, fact or opinion, emotions, or when receiving directions.
21. When listening for information in class or lectures; pay attention, ask questions, and take notes.

22. Choose a story you like.
    Know the story.
    Understand the characters involved.
    Use colorful words and expressions.
    Pause whenever necessary for effect.
    Use pitch and stress.
23. Tense is used to indicate the time an action or condition happened or existed. Tense is indicated by the addition of inflections, the use of principal parts of verbs, and the use of auxiliary verbs.
24. did
25. will melt
26. a. will know
    b. have been
27. have worked
28. will have finished
29. true
30. false
31. false
32. false
33. true
34. true

ALTERNATE LIFEPAC TEST

1. communication
2. a. feelings
   b. attitudes
3. a. pitch
   b. stress
   c. juncture
4. a. kindness
   b. anger
   c. fear
5. larynx
6. a. rise
   b. fall
7. junctures
8. bouquet
9. c
10. d
11. h
12. i
13. g
14. j
15. a
16. e
17. b
18. f
19. a. regular
    b. irregular
20. a. present
    b. past
    c. present perfect
    d. past perfect
    or future
       future perfect
21. a. passive
    b. purposeful
    c. critical
    d. appreciation
22. a. high
    b. low
23. Example:
    When God spoke, the worlds were formed.
    Power was manifest in the spoken word.
    The spoken word can comfort or hurt a
    listener.
24. Example:
    Intonations help us clarify and emphasize the
    meanings of our words. These intonations are
    called stress, pitch, and juncture.

25. Any order; any five:
    – Choose a story you enjoy.
    – Know the story and the order of its events.
    – Understand the character traits of the
      people involved.
    – Use colorful words and expressions to
      reveal feelings and attitudes or for special
      effect.
    – Pause whenever necessary to emphasize a
      word or phrase.
    – Use pitch and stress to lend variety and
      meaning to your voice.
26. Example:
    Purposeful listening should be used when
    announcements are made, directions are
    given, or information is presented.
27. blew
28. ran
29. tell
30. wore
31. a. saw
    b. was
32. true
33. true
34. false
35. false
36. true
37. true

SPELLING TEST

1	propaganda	His speech was just political **propaganda**.	propaganda
2	logical	Your reasoning is not **logical**.	logical
3	evaluate	Use these ideas to **evaluate** her speech.	evaluate
4	juncture	The use of **juncture** helps emphasize ideas.	juncture
5	embarrassed	I was too **embarrassed** to come so late.	embarrassed
6	erroneous	Your information is **erroneous**.	erroneous
7	resurrection	Christ's **resurrection** is remembered at Easter.	resurrection
8	imitate	Scotty can **imitate** the call of a Baltimore oriole.	imitate
9	precise	Your scale drawing must be **precise**.	precise
10	antagonism	Try to overcome your **antagonism**.	antagonism
11	enunciate	Try to **enunciate** your words correctly.	enunciate
12	previous	It had rained the **previous** night.	previous
13	persuasion	No amount of **persuasion** will make me go.	persuasion
14	inattention	**Inattention** may result in failure.	inattention
15	interpret	Can you **interpret** what he is saying?	interpret
16	designate	Please **designate** the time and place for the meeting.	designate
17	appropriate	It is **appropriate** to wear a tie to the meeting.	appropriate
18	lying	The cat was **lying** on a chair.	lying
19	emphasize	You should **emphasize** key ideas in your speech.	emphasize
20	bankruptcy	The man had to claim **bankruptcy**.	bankruptcy
21	technical	**Technical** words are sometimes confusing.	technical
22	mayonnaise	Do you prefer **mayonnaise** or mustard?	mayonnaise
23	catalogue	I want to order a radio from this **catalogue**.	catalogue
24	parallel	Are those lines **parallel**?	parallel
25	becoming	The room was **becoming** quiet when the bell rang.	becoming

SPELLING TEST

26	omelet	Would you like an **omelet** or scrambled eggs?	omelet
27	icing	The chocolate **icing** is delicious.	icing
28	granddaughter	Is Ellen your **granddaughter**?	granddaughter
29	academy	Hubbard is an **academy** for boys.	academy
30	foreigner	You would be a **foreigner** in another country.	foreigner
31	sandwich	I brought a peanut butter **sandwich**.	sandwich
32	bazaar	Sally brought a dollar to the **bazaar**.	bazaar
33	procedure	A special **procedure** was used for diagnosis.	procedure
34	recommend	I **recommend** the chicken for lunch.	recommend
35	disastrous	The results of the storm was **disastrous**.	disastrous
36	whether	**Whether** it rains or not, we will go to town.	whether
37	athlete	Babe Ruth was a famous **athlete**.	athlete
38	original	Send the copy and save the **original**.	original
39	earnest	Matt is very **earnest** about his beliefs.	earnest
40	definite	You should pick a **definite** time for studying.	definite
41	grammar	Using proper **grammar** is very important.	grammar
42	studying	Chris is **studying** his spelling.	studying
43	weather	My dog does not like stormy **weather**.	weather
44	muscle	Gary has a **muscle** cramp in his leg.	muscle
45	similar	Her dress is **similar** to Leah's.	similar
46	candidate	Joe is a **candidate** for class president.	candidate
47	temperament	Jeff has an excitable **temperament**.	temperament
48	balance	I can't keep my **balance** on ice skates.	balance

LANGUAGE ARTS 702

ALTERNATE LIFEPAC TEST

NAME _____

DATE _____

SCORE _____

104
130

Complete these statements (each answer, 3 points).

1. Speech is a very important tool of _____ .

2. Intonations help express a. _____ and b._____ .

3. Three intonations are a. _____ , b. _____ , and c. _____ .

4. Three character traits the tone of your voice can reveal are a. _____ , b. _____ , and c. _____ .

5. Pitch is controlled in the _____ .

6. Pitch is the a. _____ and b._____ of voice tone.

7. Pauses between sounds or words are called _____ .

8. Our voices can blend together as beautifully as a(n) _____ of mixed flowers.

Match these items (each answer, 2 points).

9. _____ vocal folds   a. the rise and fall of voice

10. _____ stress   b. propaganda

11. _____ conjugation   c. larynx

12. _____ auxiliary   d. verbal force

13. _____ tense   e. occurs automatically

14. _____ juncture   f. stress, pitch, and juncture

15. _____ pitch   g. time an action takes place

16. _____ listening   h. systematic arrangement of forms of a verb

17. _____ critical listening   i. a helping verb

18. _____ intonation   j. pause between sounds, words, or phrases

List the following items (each part, 2 points).

19. Two classifications of verbs:

    a. _____

    b. _____

20. Four tenses of verbs:

    a. _____

    b. _____

    c. _____

    d. _____

21. Four kinds of listening:

    a. _____

    b. _____

    c. _____

    d. _____

22. Two kinds of pitches:

    a. _____

    b. _____

Complete these activities (each answer, 5 points).

23. Explain why *speech* is one of God's unique gifts.

    _____

    _____

    _____

    _____

    _____

    _____

24. Explain how intonation helps us speak with more expression.

    _____

    _____

    _____

    _____

    _____

    _____

25. Explain some points to remember when telling a story. Include at least five.

    _____

    _____

    _____

    _____

    _____

    _____

26. Explain what is meant by purposeful listening.

_____

_____

_____

_____

_____

_____

Write the correct verb form (each answer, 3 points).

27. The wind (blow) _____ very hard last night.

28. The boy (run) _____ very fast in the race.

29. Please (told) _____ me what you plan to do tomorrow.

30. Alice (wear) _____ a blue dress to the party.

31. When I (see) a. _____ John, I knew he (be) b. _____ happy.

Answer *true* **or** *false* (each answer, 1 point).

32. _____ The word *hit* could be a verb or a noun.

33. _____ Verb endings are known as inflections.

34. _____ The auxiliary verb *be* is the regular verb in English.

35. _____ Listening is not an active skill.

36. _____ Intonations help clarify the meanings of our verbs.

37. _____ The future tense is used for actions that will occur in the future.

ALTERNATE SPELLING TEST

1	omelet	My brother likes eggs fried, but I like an **omelet** better.	omelet
2	icing	The **icing** on the wedding cake was white and blue.	icing
3	granddaughter	This is Sharon, Mr. Green's **granddaughter**.	granddaughter
4	academy	I want to attend a military **academy** when I'm older.	academy
5	foreigner	Ruth was a **foreigner** in her mother-in-law's homeland.	foreigner
6	sandwich	My favorite **sandwich** is ham and cheese on rye.	sandwich
7	bazaar	Rachel won a stuffed animal at the town **bazaar**.	bazaar
8	procedure	What is the **procedure** for transferring to a new district?	procedure
9	recommend	The doctor might **recommend** that he move to a cooler climate.	recommend
10	disastrous	She mixed too much pepper in the soup and the results were **disastrous**.	disastrous
11	whether	I don't know **whether** to call my mother or not.	whether
12	athlete	A famous **athlete** autographed our baseball.	athlete
13	original	Her short stories are **original** and entertaining.	original
14	earnest	I'm not teasing you; I'm in **earnest**.	earnest
15	definite	There is a **definite** difference between oranges and tangerines.	definite
16	grammar	A knowledge of **grammar** is important for all students.	grammar
17	studying	**Studying** for tests helps insure good scores.	studying
18	weather	This hot **weather** is perfect for swimming.	weather
19	muscle	What do you call the **muscle** in the front forearm?	muscle
20	similar	That poem is **similar** to another that I've read.	similar
21	candidate	I wonder who the Republican **candidate** will be?	candidate
22	temperament	She needs to develop a more cheerful **temperament**.	temperament
23	balance	Mother says that if I want a checking account, I have to **balance** it.	balance
24	propaganda	Commercials are a form of **propaganda**.	propaganda
25	logical	He drew a **logical** conclusion from the evidence.	logical

ALTERNATE SPELLING TEST

26	convey	His words **convey** a different message than his smile does.	convey
27	temporary	My sister has a **temporary** job in a bookstore.	temporary
28	fortunate	It's **fortunate** that I have a copy of the book you lost.	fortunate
29	appreciate	I **appreciate** your courtesy in answering my call.	appreciate
30	impatience	Sue doesn't hide her **impatience** well, does she?	impatience
31	relationship	My **relationship** with my brother has improved lately.	relationship
32	premise	I'm not sure that I agree with that **premise**.	premise
33	structure	Sentence **structure** is too important to be ignored.	structure
34	persuaded	Michelle finally **persuaded** David to attend the meeting.	persuaded
35	oblivious	Linda is **oblivious** to everything when she's reading.	oblivious
36	woolly	His new puppy is as **woolly** as a lamb.	woolly
37	zoology	My aunt has a degree in **zoology**.	zoology
38	knowledge	The **knowledge** that he had passed the test made him happy.	knowledge
39	villain	Fagin is the **villain** in Oliver Twist.	villain
40	yacht	I wonder how much it costs to buy a **yacht**.	yacht
41	judgment	Never pass **judgment** on others for their mistakes.	judgment
42	quite	The collie is **quite** gentle, but the poodle is not.	quite
43	desperate	Hunger made the child **desperate** enough to beg.	desperate
44	abridgment	This book is an **abridgment** of that one.	abridgment
45	nickel	Nothing costs a **nickel** anymore.	nickel
46	accompaniment	The piano **accompaniment** is too loud.	accompaniment
47	until	I can't wait **until** it's time to eat dessert.	until
48	really	Dragons never **really** existed, did they?	really
49	technical	That book is too **technical** for me.	technical
50	parallel	Pamela is as skilled as an acrobat on the **parallel** bars.	parallel

LANGUAGE ARTS 703

Unit 3: Biographies

TEACHER NOTES

MATERIALS NEEDED FOR LIFEPAC	
Required	Suggested
None	• King James Version of the Bible • dictionary or a thesaurus • reference books or online sources

ADDITIONAL LEARNING ACTIVITIES

Section 1: Biographies and Sequence of Events

1. Present problems requiring that the student draw logical conclusions from facts presented. Example: On the board write: "If the temperature is below 80°, Alice will refuse to swim. This afternoon it is 75°. What logical conclusion can you draw?" (Alice will not swim.) Or write: "If a student is tardy to English class he is marked absent. Bill was marked absent today. What logical conclusion can you draw?" (None)

2. Have a panel discussion about William Tyndale and his beliefs and contributions. Students may wish to look up more information about him.

3. Write the sequence of events of the "Parable of the Invitation to the Great Banquet" in proper order. Read the "Parable of the Invitation to the Great Banquet" in a Bible (Luke 14:16-24). The events of this parable have been listed but they are not in the proper order. Decide the correct order of the events and write the letters in the blank spaces provided.

   a. One said, "I have bought five yoke of oxen, and I go to prove them; I pray thee, have me excused."

   b. There was still room so the master told his servant to compel more people to come to his house.

   c. A man once gave a banquet and when all was ready, he sent his servants to tell all who were invited.

   d. The man was very angry and told his servant to go through the city and invite the poor and maimed and blind and lame.

   e. The man said, "None of those men which were bidden shall taste of my supper."

   f. One said, "I have bought a piece of ground, and I must needs and see it: I pray thee, have me excused."

g. One said, "I have married a wife, and therefore I cannot come."

First event: c

Second event: f

Third event: a

Fourth event: g

Fifth event: d

Sixth event: b

Seventh event: e

4. Write the sequence of events of the "Parable of the Invitation to the Wedding Feast" in proper order. Read the "Parable of the Invitation to the Wedding Feast" in a Bible (Matthew 22:2-14). The events of this parable have been listed, but they are not in the proper order. Decide the correct order of the events and write the letters in the blank spaces provided.

a. The invited guests ignored the servants, and others killed them.

b. One of the guests had no wedding garment.

c. A king gave a marriage feast for his son, and sent his servants to call those who were invited, but they would not come.

d. The king told his servants to invite anybody they could find.

e. The king had the guest tied up and cast out, saying, "For many are called, but few are chosen."

f. Again, he sent other servants to tell those who were invited that everything was ready.

g. The king was angry and sent his troops to destroy these murderers and burn their city.

First event: c

Second event: f

Third event: a

Fourth event: g

Fifth event: d

Sixth event: b

Seventh event: e

Section 2: Prefixes and Suffixes

1. Write a series of words to be analyzed.

    comprehension – seize, grasp (com/prehen/sion)

    debate – to beat (de/bate)

    chronological – reasoning (chrono/logic/al)

    prejudicial – judgment (pre/judic/ial).

    Give the meaning of each root and let students figure the meanings of the entire word from their knowledge of prefixes and suffixes.

2. Give each group a list of five roots. Each group will add prefixes and suffixes to each root to form a new word. The group with the most words wins.

    Example words:

    serve

    press

    scribe

    bank

    family (familia)

3. Find a short newspaper or magazine article. Mark all prefixes and suffixes in colored ink. Display in room.

4. Make a prefix or suffix wheel with root or base words in the inner circle and prefixes or suffixes in the outer circle. Spin until you have formed a list of ten words. You may want to have a contest with a friend to see who can put together the most words in a certain time frame (three minutes).

Administer the LIFEPAC Spelling Test.

The test is provided in this Teacher's Guide.

Evaluate the tests and review the words the students spelled incorrectly.

If necessary, review all of the words in the unit to prepare for the alternate spelling test.

Administer the Alternate LIFEPAC Spelling test that is provided in this Teacher's Guide.

Administer the LIFEPAC Test.

The test is to be administered in one session. Give no help except with directions.

Evaluate the tests and review areas where the students have done poorly.

Review the pages and activities that stress the concepts tested.

If necessary, administer the Alternate LIFEPAC Test.

ANSWER KEYS

SECTION 1

1.1   a form of literary prose, closely related to history, attempting to describe a specific individual in a specific time and place

1.2   to give the reader an understanding of the personality of the person and a factual sequence of events influenced by his period in history

1.3   Biblical accounts of patriarchs, Gospel accounts of Jesus Christ, early Roman and Greek philosophers, religious biographies and biographies of martyrs and saints

1.4   James Boswell's *Life of Samuel Johnson*.

1.5   Political and religious biographies— Carl Sandburg's *Abraham Lincoln*.

1.6   An author's written account of his own life.

1.7   A personal record of events the author has witnessed or experienced.

1.8   c

1.9   b

1.10   d

1.11   c

1.12   a

1.13   Brussels

1.14   1536

1.15   a. He helped and encouraged refugees from England.
    b. He tried to help the poor.
    or He dared to spread the Gospel in his own way despite the dangers to himself.

1.16   Latin

1.17   Any order:
    a. pay a fine
    b. go to prison
    c. be burned at the stake as heretics

1.18   Either order:
    a. King Henry VIII
    b. Martin Luther

1.19   While in prison, he asked for his Hebrew Bible, Hebrew grammar, and Hebrew dictionary.

1.20   So everyone who spoke English could read God's Holy Word.

1.21   a. Tyndale disappeared and probably went to Wittenberg University. (Paragraph 17)
    b. Tyndale escaped to Worms and finished his translation of the New Testament. (Paragraph 22)
    c. William Tyndale made friends with a young Englishman named Henry Phillips. (Paragraph 25)
    d. Four months later William Tyndale was burned at the stake. (Paragraph 29)

1.22   Teacher check

1.23   b

1.24   c

1.25   b

1.26   c

1.27   a

1.28   c

1.29   c

1.30   a

1.31   a

1.32   a

1.33-1.42 Examples:

1.33   heretic –
    He was wrongly accused of being a *heretic*.

1.34   martyr –
    William Tyndale was a Christian *martyr*.

1.35   infer –
    You can *infer* a great deal from the information you have.

1.36   hinder –
    Poor spelling can *hinder* your progress in school.

1.37   amid –
    One petunia stood *amid* the daisies.

1.38   biography –
    Have you ever read a *biography* of George Washington?

1.39   patriotic –
    Dolley Madison was a *patriotic* woman.

1.40   Friends –
    The Quakers called themselves *Friends*.

1.41 autobiography –
"The Story of My Life" is an *autobiography* by Helen Keller.

1.42 courage –
Dolley Madison showed great *courage* in spite of her danger.

1.43 c

1.44 b

1.45 c

1.46 c

1.47 a

1.48 She said that she loved everybody.

1.49
a. national treasures including the Declaration of Independence
b. a famous Gilbert Stuart painting of George Washington

1.50 1814

1.51 A messenger told her that the British wanted to capture Mr. and Mrs. Madison and take them back to London in chains.

1.52 twenty-one years

1.53 An action or event is revealed later than it would have been if a chronological order had been used. It usually explains something in the present by revealing something in the past.

1.54
a. Information is revealed through the character's memory.
b. Another character tells about a past event.
c. The author gives the information directly.

1.55
a. After the Revolutionary War, her family moved to Philadelphia.
(Paragraphs 4-5)
b. Three years later, her husband died.
(Paragraph 7)
c. James Madison became Secretary of State and President Jefferson asked Dolly to be a hostess for dinners at the White House.
(Paragraph 13)
d. In 1812, a war broke out between the United States and England.
(Paragraph 15)
e. Dolley Madison packed the nation's most valuable papers as the British began to enter the city.
(Paragraphs 18-20)
f. At the last moment she also took a famous painting of George Washington and escaped just in time.
(Paragraphs 21-23)
g. The war was over the next year and the state papers and the painting of Washington were returned to the capitol.
(Paragraph 25)

1.56
a. 1814
b. the next year *or* 1815
c. five years earlier *or* 1809

1.57 Teacher check

1.58
a. The son journeyed to a far country and wasted all his money on riotous living.
b. He took a job feeding pigs and ate some of their food to stay alive.
c. When he returned, his father showed great compassion and gave him clothes and had the servants prepare a feast.
d. The elder son told his father he was angry because he had been loyal to his father but no party had ever been given for him.

1.59 Any order:

le words		*el* words
a. puzzle		i. angel
b. angle		j. label
c. temple		k. nickel
d. trickle		
e. pickle		
f. icicle		
g. profitable		
h. parable		

1.60
a. meaning
b. order
c. residents *or* dwellers
d. gainful
e. method

SELF TEST 1

1.01 English
1.02 Brussels
1.03 Martin Luther
1.04 autobiography
1.05 Quaker
1.06 being First Lady and acting First Lady; White House hostess
1.07 saving important documents and the Stuart painting of Washington from the invading British
1.08 Either order:
a. Old Testament patriarchs
b. Gospel accounts of Jesus Christ
1.09 the order in which events occur in a story
1.010 the order in which the actions occur during an event
1.011 a form of literary prose, closely related to history, attempting to describe a specific individual in a specific time and place
1.012 an action or event revealed later than it would have in chronological order
1.013 a process of reasoning in which a particular conclusion must result from the known facts
1.014 recollections or observations of the times or events a person has witnessed
1.015 d
1.016 g
1.017 a
1.018 e
1.019 i
1.020 f
1.021 h
1.022 c
1.023 c
1.024 b
1.025 e
1.026 a
1.027 d
1.028 a
1.029 a

SECTION 2

2.1
a. de | part
b. un | true
c. ex | change
d. fore | arm
e. en | able
f. in | correct
g. mega | ton
h. mis | take
i. non | sense
j. per | form
k. re | turn
l. super | man
m. under | feed
n. trans | plant
o. un | kind
p. dis | appear
q. intra | state
r. dis | like
s. ad | verb

2.2 Examples; any order:
a. aircraft
b. gravity
c. freeze
d. social

2.3 Examples; any order:
a. pay
b. turn
c. call
d. play

2.4 Examples; any order:
a. certain
b. holy
c. even
d. true

2.5 Examples; any order:
a. take
b. use
c. lead
d. behave

2.6 Word puzzle:

```
C O O P E R A T E M R I F N O C
I O N I A T R E C N U M E R P O
R E M M P O S T D A T E R T A N
C S U P E R N A T U R A L L R R
U A R L I N T A K E R E E L A E
M E N A X L R E P L A Y E E C D
N C O N I D E N X R L E S P H I
A E R T F I N I T R U L N S U S
V D R Y E S I R O O G R E S T A
I N T E R C H A N G E N S I E G
G R E N P H A M O O R E N M O R
A R T F R A M B L Y R I O N R E
T G O D X R I U N P I C N O R E
E N E R G G O S E N N D O U B R
B I L E V E L D D I S O B E Y E
```

a. dis-   m. super-
b. de-   n. circum-
c. un-   o. dis-
d. inter-   p. co-
e. dis-   q. com-
f. para-   r. im-
g. in-   s. re-
h. post-   t. de-
i. con-   u. ir-
j. pre-   v. non-
k. bi-   w. mis-
l. sub-   x. in-

2.7 Teacher check
2.8 a. compose
       b. depose
       c. interpose
       d. propose
2.9 a. autograph
       b. photograph
       c. biograph(y)
       d. telegraph
       e. phonograph
2.10 a. biennial
        b. triennial
        c. centennial
        d. hexennial
2.11 a. contradict
        b. edict
        c. predict
        d. verdict
        e. benedict

2.12 a. chronometer
        b. diameter
        c. micrometer
        d. perimeter
        e. thermometer
2.13 a. art | ist
        b. rest | less
        c. time | ly
        d. treat | ment
        e. act | or
        f. need | ed
        g. sad | ness
        h. hand | ful
        i. even | ly
        j. eat | ing
        k. king | dom
        l. fast | est
        m. self | ish
        n. class | ic
        o. person | al
        p. pass | age
        q. wood | en
        r. help | er
        s. man | hood

2.14
Use	Meaning
a. noun	b. one who wishes
c. adjective	d. full of wishing
e. verb	f. action of wishing; wanting

2.15
Use	Meaning
a. noun	b. one who helps
c. adjective	d. full of help
e. adjective	f. without help
g. verb	h. action of helping; aiding

2.16
Use	Meaning
a. adjective	b. like a man
c. adjective/adverb	d. like a man
e. noun	f. condition of being a man

2.17
Word	Use
a. humorist	b. noun
c. humorless	d. adjective
e. humorous	f. adjective

2.18
Word	Use
a. correctly	b. adverb
c. correctness	d. noun
e. correction	f. noun
g. correctable	h. adjective

2.19
Word	Use
a. agreeable	b. adjective
c. agreement	d. noun
e. agreeing	f. verb

2.20 Any order:
a. -er
b. -ness
c. -en
d. -ing
e. -ly

2.21 Any order:
a. -able
b. -r
c. -dom
d. -ing
e. -ly

2.22 Any order:
a. -able
b. -er
c. -ing
d. -age

2.23 Word puzzle:

D	B	A	C	K	W	A	R	D	O	R	N	P	E	G
E	I	A	R	M	F	U	L	I	N	T	E	R	O	L
T	G	O	D	I	F	F	E	R	E	N	T	O	R	O
R	N	O	O	L	T	R	I	T	M	R	A	F	L	O
A	E	N	T	G	Y	L	X	Y	W	E	D	I	U	M
P	S	O	N	G	R	R	Y	R	O	N	I	T	F	Y
M	S	I	R	E	N	N	A	M	R	I	U	A	P	R
G	O	V	E	R	N	M	E	N	T	S	Q	B	L	E
G	F	U	T	C	I	O	R	E	H	U	I	L	E	F
W	I	S	H	F	U	L	R	N	L	O	L	E	H	R
T	W	I	I	R	S	S	E	L	E	R	A	C	R	E
T	R	T	R	O	U	B	L	E	S	O	M	E	E	E
A	L	U	F	E	P	O	H	O	S	G	R	R	N	D
C	A	R	B	O	N	A	T	E	N	I	N	N	E	O
C	O	N	F	E	S	S	I	O	N	V	R	O	O	M

a. -ful   m. -ment
b. -ward   n. -ful
c. -ly   o. -ic
d. -ness   p. -ful
e. -ate   q. -ate
f. -less   r. -ism
g. -ion   s. -ed
h. -ent   t. -able
i. -y   u. -some
j. -dom   v. -ous
k. -y   w. -ful
l. -ing   x. -less

2.24 name of the person who worked the puzzle

2.25
a. dentist
b. sophist
c. oculist

2.26
a. civic
b. graphic
c. metric

2.27.
a. dermal
b. medial
c. vocal
d. thermal
e. final
f. visual
g. mortal
h. verbal

2.28
a. durable
b. portable

2.29
a. flexible
b. credible
c. audible
d. visible

2.30
a. con-
b. solid
c. -ate

2.31
a. mis-
b. treat
c. -ment

2.32
a. un-
b. even
c. -ly

2.33
a. inter-
b. change
c. -able

2.34
a. col-
b. labor
c. -ate

2.35
a. un-
b. hero
c. -ic

2.36
a. dis-
b. respect
c. -ful

2.37
a. con-
b. current
c. -ly

2.38
a. in-
b. habit
c. -ant

2.39
a. in-
b. vigor
c. -ate

2.40
a. de-
b. magnet
c. -ize

2.41
a. out-
b. land
c. -ish

2.42 a. de-
b. human
c. -ize

2.43 a. un-
b. world
c. -ly

2.44 a. trans-
b. ocean
c. -ic

2.45 Word puzzle:

R	E	N	U	M	B	E	R	I	N	G	R	R	A	N	T	G	R		
E	E	U	N	M	I	N	D	F	U	L	X	T	O	R	M	N	Y		
F	E	D	R	U	L	L	A	N	O	S	R	E	P	M	I	I	Z		
R	R	D	E	N	B	I	A	N	N	U	A	L	L	Y	S	D	N		
E	N	I	S	P	T	N	E	M	E	N	I	F	E	R	M	N	O		
S	R	S	T	A	O	P	P	R	R	E	E	N	N	Y	A	E	R		
H	E	A	F	Y	O	S	A	D	J	U	S	T	M	E	N	T	P		
M	S	G	U	A	G	N	I	T	N	A	L	P	E	R	A	N	E		
E	E	R	L	B	M	U	L	T	I	P	L	Y	I	N	G	I	R		
N	A	E	L	L	L	L	I	I	N	N	Z	Z	E	E	F		F		
T	R	E	T	E	S	T	E	D	N	N	P	P	R	R	S	S	O		
C	C	A	A	P	P	G	G	R	R	G	G	I	I	N	N	R	R		
H	H	B	R	E	H	P	A	R	G	O	T	O	H	P	P	M	M		
X	I	L	L	E	G	A	L	L	Y	L	A	M	R	O	N	B	A		
N	N	E	E	D	D	Y	Y	L	T	N	E	S	B	A	R	R	N		
G	G	D	E	P	R	E	S	S	I	O	N	A	A	D	D	C	C		
O	O	T	T	M	M	I	S	S	P	E	L	L	I	N	G	I	E		

a. <u>dis</u>-agree-<u>able</u>
b. <u>bi</u>-annual-<u>ly</u>
c. <u>re</u>-deposit-<u>ing</u>
d. <u>re</u>-fine-<u>ment</u>
e. <u>per</u>-form-<u>ance</u>
f. <u>re</u>-fresh-<u>ment</u>
g. <u>photo</u>-graph-<u>er</u>
h. <u>ad</u>-just-<u>ment</u>
i. <u>il</u>-legal-<u>ly</u>
j. <u>mis</u>-man-<u>age</u>
k. <u>un</u>-mind-<u>ful</u>
l. <u>ab</u>-norm-<u>al</u>

m. <u>re</u>-number-<u>ing</u>
n. <u>un</u>-pay-<u>able</u>
o. <u>im</u>-person-<u>al</u>
p. <u>re</u>-plant-<u>ing</u>
q <u>multi</u>-ply-<u>ing</u>
r. <u>de</u>-press-<u>ion</u>
s. <u>un</u>-rest-<u>ful</u>
t. <u>re</u>-search-<u>ing</u>
u. <u>ab</u>-sent-<u>ly</u>
v. <u>mis</u>-spell-<u>ing</u>
w. <u>in</u>-tend-<u>ing</u>
x. <u>re</u>-test-<u>ed</u>

2.46 c
2.47 a
2.48 b
2.49 d
2.50 b
2.51 c
2.52 d
2.53 a
2.54 a
2.55 d
2.56 b
2.57 b

SELF TEST 2

2.01   deduce
2.02   heretic
2.03   martyr
2.04   autobiography
2.05   memoirs
2.06   biography
2.07   chronological
2.08   flashback technique
2.09   prefix
2.010 suffix
2.011 He believed each person should be able
to read the Bible in English. Although they
were punishable by death, he stood by these
beliefs.
2.012 deeply religious—Quaker—nonviolent,
patriotic, courageous; risked capture by the
enemy to save valuable documents and the
Stuart painting of Washington
2.013 un | <u>like</u>
2.014 de | <u>press</u>
2.015 re | <u>pay</u>
2.016 mis | <u>treat</u>
2.017 inter | <u>play</u>
2.018 <u>truth</u> | ful
2.019 <u>appear</u> | ance
2.020 <u>state</u> | ment
2.021 <u>like</u> | ly
2.022 <u>correct</u> | ness
2.023 per | <u>form</u> | ance
2.024 dis | <u>obey</u> | ing
2.025 re | <u>turn</u> | able
2.026 com | <u>part</u> | ment
2.027 un | <u>self</u> | ish
2.028 re (form)
2.029 (therm) al
2.030 (port) er
2.031 com (pose)
2.032 re (ply) ing
2.033 replay
2.034 interchange
2.035 nonsense
2.036 return
2.037 mislead
2.038 dental
2.039 tractor
2.040 potent
2.041 portable
2.042 graphic

LIFEPAC TEST

1. dis | <u>agree</u>
2. un | <u>certain</u>
3. post | <u>date</u>
4. de | <u>press</u>
5. <u>fool</u> | ish
6. <u>art</u> | ist *or* <u>ar</u> | tist
7. <u>rest</u> | less
8. <u>treat</u> | ment
9. con | <u>solid</u> | ate
10. dis | <u>appear</u> | ing
11. re | <u>do</u> | ing
12. anti-
13. inter-
14. mis-
15. im-
16. re-
17. interpose
18. contradict
19. inscribe
20. centennial
21. thermometer

22.-24.	Word		Part of Speech
22.	a. helper	b.	noun
23.	a. passable	b.	adjective
24.	a. correctly	b.	adverb

25. d
26. e
27. c
28. a
29. d
30. e
31. b
32. e
33. d
34. a
35. b
36. b

ALTERNATE LIFEPAC TEST

1. inter | <u>change</u>
2. bi | <u>level</u>
3. dis | <u>obey</u>
4. non | <u>sense</u>
5. <u>sad</u> | ness
6. <u>hand</u> | ful
7. <u>man</u> | hood
8. <u>fast</u> | est
9. un | <u>self</u> | ish
10. in | <u>correct</u> | ly
11. over | <u>power</u> | ing
12. re-
13. mis-
14. anti-
15. inter-
16. im-
17. compose
18. verdict
19. autograph
20. biennial
21. chronometer

22.-24.	Word		Part of Speech
22.	a. lighter	b.	noun
23.	a. lightly	b.	adverb
24.	a. lightable	b.	adjective

25. c
26. d
27. b
28. a
29. b
30. d
31. translating the Bible into English
32. a. saving the Declaration of Independence and government documents
    b. saving the portrait of George Washington
33. Dolley Madison
34. g
35. b
36. e
37. c
38. a
39. d
40. f

SPELLING TEST

1	amid	The golf ball fell **amid** the flowers behind the house.	amid
2	smuggle	Randy tried to **smuggle** his pet snake into his bedroom.	smuggle
3	infer	In his speech, he meant to **infer** that the event never occurred.	infer
4	careless	Campers were warned not to be **careless** about campfires.	careless
5	logical	Their argument seemed **logical** until more facts were brought out.	logical
6	include	Why not **include** an apple in the lunch pail?	include
7	torturous	The pain was **torturous** when my brother broke his leg.	torturous
8	famous	San Francisco is **famous** for its trolleys.	famous
9	purify	A good way to **purify** water is to boil it.	purify
10	pickle	The old **pickle** jar was still sitting in the pantry.	pickle
11	parable	By using the **parable**, Jesus taught many basic truths.	parable
12	strength	A nation's **strength** is measured in the morality of its people.	strength
13	sequence	The pictures had been in the right **sequence** before they fell on the floor.	sequence
14	witty	John could be counted on for a **witty** remark.	witty
15	persecution	Christians and Jews have suffered much **persecution** over the centuries.	persecution
16	chronological	Arrange these historical events in **chronological** order.	chronological
17	patriotic	Many **patriotic** songs were played at the celebration.	patriotic
18	vineyard	Workers in the **vineyard** spent long hours harvesting the grapes.	vineyard
19	temple	Jesus drove money changers from the **temple**.	temple
20	interpose	The coach had to **interpose** himself between the two struggling boys.	interpose
21	humorless	No one expected a **humorless** speech from the school principal.	humorless
22	natural	The store sold **natural** foods in many different forms.	natural
23	prayer	Every evening our family had a time of **prayer** before bedtime.	prayer

SPELLING TEST

24	puzzle	Putting the **puzzle** together was easy for the first graders.	puzzle
25	confirm	The store had to **confirm** the purchase with Andy's parents.	confirm
26	loot	Armies often **loot** abandoned cities that they capture.	loot
27	biography	Reading the **biography** of Thomas Jefferson was our assignment.	biography
28	courage	It takes **courage** to witness for Jesus Christ.	courage
29	nickel	A **nickel** does not buy as much as it did ten years ago.	nickel·
30	misjudge	The driver said it was easy to **misjudge** the curve in the road.	misjudge
31	fanciful	Nancy remembered the **fanciful** stories her mother used to tell her.	fanciful
32	emit	The radio started to **emit** a strange noise.	emit
33	angle	Looking at the problem from a different **angle** helped him to solve it.	angle
34	tenants	Most of the apartment **tenants** were elderly people.	tenants
35	hinder	Danny did not wish to **hinder** his teammates.	hinder
36	autobiography	The last **autobiography** he read was the longest one.	autobiography
37	government	County **government** officials inspected the property.	government
38	icicle	Only one **icicle** was left hanging from the roof.	icicle
39	prettiest	A prize for the **prettiest** flower basket was won by Carol.	prettiest
40	lighten	Extra help was needed to **lighten** the heavy load they carried.	lighten
41	tuning	Grace had an easy time **tuning** her guitar.	tuning
42	centennial	Plans for the **centennial** celebration included a band contest.	centennial
43	angel	The first chapter of Luke tells of the **angel** Gabriel.	angel
44	flashback	Some stories use **flashback** to tell about previous events.	flashback
45	Brussels	The capital of Belgium is **Brussels**, the largest city in the country.	Brussels
46	memoirs	Famous people usually write **memoirs** about their experiences.	memoirs

SPELLING TEST

47	conclusions	You can draw your own **conclusions** after the debate ends.	conclusions
48	technique	It required a certain **technique** to produce the right effect in the photograph.	technique
49	refugee	A Vietnamese **refugee** told of the suffering in his country.	refugee
50	deduce	We could **deduce** from the evidence which person was telling the truth.	deduce

LANGUAGE ARTS 703

ALTERNATE LIFEPAC TEST

NAME _____

DATE _____

SCORE _____

84

105

Draw a line under the base word in each longer word and a vertical line (up and down) between the prefix and the base word (each numbered answer, 2 points).

1. interchange

2. bilevel

3. disobey

4. nonsense

Draw a line under the base word in each longer word and a vertical line between the suffix and the base word (each numbered answer, 2 points).

5. sadness

6. handful

7. manhood

8. fastest

Draw a line under the base word and a vertical line between the prefix and base word and another vertical line between the base word and the suffix (each numbered answer, 2 points).

9. unselfish

10. incorrectly

11. overpowering

Add the correct prefix. Study the list of prefixes and their definitions. Add the correct prefix to each base word by using the definition of the word as a guide (each answer, 2 points).

im- = not	inter- = between	re- = back, again
mis- = bad, wrongly	anti- = against	

12. _____ do (do again)

13. _____ treat (treat wrongly)

14. _____ matter (against matter)

15. _____ change (change between)

16. _____ perfect (not perfect)

Write the correct words in the blank spaces. Use the lists of prefixes and roots with the meanings of each (each answer, 2 points).

Prefix	Root
com- = together	dict = speak
auto- = self	pose = put
chrono- = time	ennial = year
ver- = truth	graph = write
bi- = two	meter = measure

17. put together = _____

18. speak truth = _____

19. self writing = _____

20. two years = _____

21. time measure = _____

Write the correct words in the blank spaces. Use the list of suffixes, their meanings, and the parts of speech indicated (each answer, 3 points).

Suffix	Meaning	Part of Speech
-able	able	adjective
-er	a person who, or thing that does	noun
-ly	manner	adverb

	Definition	Word	Part of Speech
22.	a thing that *lights*	a. _____	b. _____
23.	in a *light* manner	a. _____	b. _____
24.	able to *light*	a. _____	b. _____

Write the correct letter (each answer, 2 points).

25. When an author explains a present situation by going back to an earlier event he is using _____ .

a. foreshadowing

b. chronological sequence

c. flashback technique

d. sequence of events

26. Personal records of experiences or events the writer has witnessed are called _____ .

a. witticisms

b. biographies

c. sequences

d. memoirs

27. Another word for *inference* is _____ .

a. knowledge

b. deduction

c. persecution

d. heretic

28. An answer that is not directly stated may result from _____ .

a. drawing logical conclusions

b. guessing

c. suggestions

d. using the flashback technique

29. Jill discovers an old box in the attic. She takes it to her room. Her mother tells her about the things she packed away in it long before Jill was born.

The preceding paragraph is an example of _____ .

a. foreshadowing

b. flashback

c. sequence of events

d. chronological sequence

30. Johnny hears a knock at the door. He opens the door. His aunt Hilda hands him a box. He opens the box and says, "Thank you for the birthday present."

The preceding paragraph is an example of _____ .

a. foreshadowing

b. sequence of events

c. logical conclusion

d. b and c

Complete these statements (each answer, 3 points).

31. The major contribution by William Tyndale was _____

_____ .

32. Dolly Madison is known for a. _____

_____ and

b. _____ .

33. The person who grew up as a Quaker was _____ .

Write the letter to show the sequence of events in proper order (each answer, 3 points).

34. _____   a. The trunks were loaded on the carriage.

35. _____   b. President Madison left Washington.

36. _____   c. A messenger announced the arrival of the British in Washington.

37. _____   d. Dolley Madison got the painting of George Washington.

38. _____   e. Dolley Madison packed her trunks with documents.

39. _____   f. The carriage left the White House as the British Army arrived.

40. _____   g. The British landed near Washington.

ALTERNATE SPELLING TEST

1	declaration	The mayor's **declaration** of policy appeared in the newspaper.	declaration
2	correctly	Most people **correctly** predicted the outcome of the game.	correctly
3	torturous	Marching through the jungle was a **torturous** experience.	torturous
4	definition	Mike forgot the **definition** of one word.	definition
5	opposite	The two sisters sat **opposite** one another at the table.	opposite
6	pickle	One **pickle** jar was left in the refrigerator.	pickle
7	frivolous	Jamie thinks ruffled dresses are **frivolous**.	frivolous
8	enemy	Satan is the **enemy** of our Lord.	enemy
9	loose-tongued	Being **loose-tongued** can cause many problems.	loose-tongued
10	friends	The **friends** had a Bible study in her home.	friends
11	impolite	He felt it was **impolite** to take the last piece of cake.	impolite
12	nickel	Some of the metals mined in Arizona are **nickel**, copper, and silver.	nickel
13	arrangement	The suggested **arrangement** favored the slower team.	arrangement
14	beautiful	Watching the **beautiful** sunset was an inspiring event.	beautiful
15	autograph	The boys tried to get the **autograph** of the famous coach.	autograph
16	strength	Exercise is a good way to increase your **strength**.	strength
17	label	The pharmacist was careful to **label** his prescription.	label
18	mysterious	No one could guess who the **mysterious** voice belonged to.	mysterious
19	freedom	To maintain **freedom**, a nation has to be strong.	freedom
20	lighten	Sailors threw cargo into the sea to **lighten** the ship's load.	lighten
21	holiness	The Bible says much about the need for **holiness** in our lives.	holiness
22	include	A good breakfast would **include** fruit juice.	include
23	Quaker	The **Quaker** movement began in the 17th Century.	Quaker
24	witty	Many **witty** sayings were printed in the magazine.	witty

ALTERNATE SPELLING TEST

25	heretic	The tour guide pointed out a place where a **heretic** died for his beliefs.	heretic
26	amid	Singing could be heard **amid** all the noise.	amid
27	profitable	Tim's paper route was as **profitable** as he had expected.	profitable
28	tenants	Finding **tenants** for the apartment was an easy matter.	tenants
29	agreeable	Everyone was **agreeable** during the entire meeting.	agreeable
30	tuning	The use of the **tuning** fork was explained by the teacher.	tuning
31	noisy	The **noisy** crowd could be heard blocks from the stadium.	noisy
32	interpose	Try to **interpose** two vehicles between the barriers.	interpose
33	martyr	Studying about the **martyr** was an interesting project.	martyr
34	patriotic	Flying the flag is a **patriotic** act on a holiday.	patriotic
35	trickle	A slow **trickle** of molasses came from the jar.	trickle
36	sequence	Paragraphs in the news story were in **sequence**.	sequence
37	hateful	They tried to refrain from developing a **hateful** attitude.	hateful
38	troublesome	Warnings were given about the **troublesome** road conditions.	troublesome
39	prayer	The **prayer** of a righteous man avails much, the Bible says.	prayer
40	logical	Her arguments seemed to be **logical** to those listening.	logical
41	icicle	As it melted, the **icicle** dripped water on the car.	icicle
42	annoying	The barking dogs were **annoying** to the neighborhood.	annoying
43	management	George was praised for his good **management** of the classroom.	management
44	circumnavigate	Portuguese sailors were noted for their ability to **circumnavigate** the earth.	circumnavigate
45	Scripture	By studying **Scripture**, you can become acquainted with God.	Scripture
46	contributions	Jewish prophets made great **contributions** to the Old Testament.	contributions

ALTERNATE SPELLING TEST

47	achievement	The teacher had hoped for more **achievement** from her class.	achievement
48	wearisome	For many early pioneers, life was **wearisome** on their prairie farms.	wearisome
49	courage	Sammy's **courage** did not fail as he raced through the dark woods.	courage
50	misjudge	The coach wondered if he could **misjudge** the opposing team.	misjudge

LANGUAGE ARTS 704

Unit 4: Structure of Language

TEACHER NOTES

MATERIALS NEEDED FOR LIFEPAC	
Required	Suggested
None	• encyclopedia or an American History book • reference books or online sources

ADDITIONAL LEARNING ACTIVITIES

Section 1: Sentence Structure and Patterns

1. Choose a poem or a paragraph from an acceptable source and write it on the board. Have students label each sentence according to structure and pattern.

2. Have a "sentence bee." Write sentences on the board and let each student have a turn at identifying specific word parts. Students missing their words should sit down.

3. Have each group prepare a presentation of one of the sentence patterns. Each group should show the pattern, provide examples (on posters or on the board), and then ask members of other groups to identify that pattern or to make up examples.

4. Choose a Biblical passage and mark the sentence pattern used. You may paste this on the bulletin board. Compile a booklet of these examples.

Section 2: Sentence Variation and Creativity

1. Write several simple, bland sentences on the board. Have the students rewrite them using a variety of patterns. See how many ways each sentence can be written or expanded.

2. Each group should read through the headlines of several newspapers or study the captions of pictures to find examples of ambiguity in meaning. These examples should be presented to the students for clarification.

3. Summarize a simple incident or description into a few colorless sentences. Now transform this incident into an interesting, informative, or exciting story by using vivid descriptive words. Remember to use a variety of sentence patterns and to avoid sentence errors. You may want to read your paper to the students.

4. Proofread another student's paper for errors and to suggest improvements.

5. Evaluate a literature selection that particularly appeals to you. Tell why it appeals to you. Is it the descriptive words, variety of sentence patterns, or clear expression of the main idea? Explain and give examples.

6. Write a creative story in which you let your imagination go. Create an impossible situation, unusual creatures, daring rescues, or whatever appeals to you.

Section 3: Sentence Meaning and Emphasis

1. Choose a poem to be read by the students. Point out the idea being expressed by the author. Ask the group to read the poem aloud, expressing this meaning by pauses and pitch variety.

2. Find a recording of an author or actor reading his works or those of another author and let the students listen to it. Ask them to comment about the meaning expressed.

3. Choose a scene of an acceptable play or a poem with at least two speaking parts. Practice reading this selection and present it to the rest of the class or to another class.

4. Write a short paragraph but do not punctuate it. Ask another person to read it aloud without reading it silently first. Was he able to show the correct meaning with his voice?

5. Choose a poem by Wordsworth, Tennyson, Longfellow, Frost, or another poet. Read this poem aloud, trying to express the meaning intended by the author.

6. Choose a Psalm to read aloud. Express the meaning by varying voice, pitch, and expression.

7. Listen to your friends. Do you hear anything unusual about the way they speak? List anything that you think is interesting.

Administer the LIFEPAC Spelling Test.
The test is provided in this Teacher's Guide.
Evaluate the tests and review the words the students spelled incorrectly.
If necessary, review all of the words in the unit to prepare for the alternate spelling test.
Administer the Alternate LIFEPAC Spelling test that is provided in this Teacher's Guide.

Administer the LIFEPAC Test.
The test is to be administered in one session. Give no help except with directions.
Evaluate the tests and review areas where the students have done poorly.
Review the pages and activities that stress the concepts tested.
If necessary, administer the Alternate LIFEPAC Test.

ANSWER KEYS

SECTION 1

1.1 <u>My grandmother</u> <u>moved away</u>.

1.2 <u>The sun</u> <u>rose at 5:00 a.m.</u>

1.3 <u>The white clouds</u> <u>drifted across the sky</u>.

1.4 <u>Steve</u> <u>ate lunch too early</u>.

1.5 <u>A squeaking noise</u> <u>came from inside the closet</u>.

1.6 <u>Mr. and Mrs. Potter</u> <u>painted their house blue</u>.

1.7 <u>plant</u> <u>bloomed</u>

1.8 <u>cars</u> <u>run</u>

1.9 <u>buttercups</u> <u>bloomed</u>

1.10 <u>storm</u> <u>raged</u>

1.11 <u>John</u> <u>went</u>

1.12 <u>Margie</u> <u>lives</u>

1.13 a group of words that communicates a complete thought

1.14 a. subject
b. predicate

1.15 a. noun
b. pronoun

1.16 verb

1.17 we would not know what the subject is doing without it.

1.18 Around the block walked my father.

1.19 Beside the lake the artist was painting.

1.20 In a hammock slept Jimmy.

1.21 Beneath the oak tree played Sara.

1.22 Around the curve roared the car.

1.23 Example:
<u>Joey</u> and <u>Jeffrey</u> love to sleep in the backyard. They <u>set</u> <u>up</u> a tent and <u>sleep</u> in sleeping bags. <u>James</u> and <u>Fred</u>, their friends, <u>come</u> over and <u>spend</u> the night with them sometimes.

1.24 the person or thing to whom or what the subject does something

1.25 a. whom
b. what

1.26 transitive

1.27 Example:
Sentences are usually more interesting when they are longer and more complex because they show more depth and variety and are more interesting to read.

1.28 shoes

1.29 garage

1.30 piano

1.31 cake

1.32 lemonade

1.33-1.34 Examples:

1.33 Mrs. Fuller made a dress and a coat.

1.34 The wind whirled the leaves and grass around the yard.

1.35-1.39 Examples:

1.35 rose

1.36 cook

1.37 sailor

1.38 John

1.39 oak

1.40 author; p.n.

1.41 interesting; p.a.

1.42 singer; p.n.

1.43 president; p.n.

1.44 neat; p.a.

1.45 false

1.46 false

1.47 true

1.48 false

1.49 Samson–*s*; gave–*v*; Philistines–*i.o.*; riddle–*d.o.*

1.50 Janelle–*s*; offered–*v*; Jennifer–*i.o.*; ride–*d.o.*

1.51 Ken–*s*; showed–*v*; Kevin–*i.o.*; skateboard–*d.o.*

1.52 Shelley–*s*; made–*v*; Donna–*i.o.*; skirt–*d.o.*

1.53 b

1.54 b

1.55 a

1.56 c

1.57 a

1.58 Sentences will vary.
Examples:
a. introduce –
I will *introduce* my friend.
b. pronounce –
Please *pronounce* my name correctly.
c. identify –
I will *identify* the winner,
d. modify –
Does an adverb *modify* a verb?
e. inverted –
Bill *inverted* the bucket of water.

1.59 <u>Across</u>

4. one
6. cot
8. verb
9. at
11. noun
12. mop
13. p.m.
14. and
15. linking
16. it
17. job
18. is
20. subject
23. an
24. ran

26. direct object
27. intransitive
31. Sarai
32. vat
33. nominative
37. sin
39. adjective
42. B.C.
44. toe
45. Ed
46. data
48. add
49. S.E.
50. inverted
51. ant

1.60 <u>Down</u>

1. compound
2. predicates
3. indirect
4. on
5. exit
7. tomb
10. ton
14. as
16. in
19. jar
20. sub
21. bee
22. transitive
25. near

28. thin
29. adverb
30. ten
34. object
35. noted
36. end
37. send
38. eat
40. Eden
41. ate
43. can
47. as
48. ad

SELF TEST 1

1.01 d
1.02 e
1.03 a
1.04 g
1.05 f
1.06 h
1.07 c
1.08 b
1.09 Either order:
a. subject
b. predicate
1.010 transitive
1.011 intransitive
1.012 b. an adjective
1.013 b. who or what the sentence is about
1.014 b. made
1.015 <u>I gazed</u>
1.016 <u>mother walked</u>
1.017 <u>Susan came</u>
1.018 b. punctuation
1.019 a. preposition
1.020 c. intransitive
1.021-1.026 Examples; any order:
<u>Action</u>
1.021 walk
1.022 run
1.023 slide
<u>Linking</u>
1.024 is
1.025 am
1.026 are
1.027 Mr. Jones–*s*; gave–*v*; Sherry–*i.o.*; A–*d.o.*
1.028 Sandy–*s*; made–*v*; cake–*d.o.*
1.029 dog–*s*; grabbed–*v*; bone–*d.o.*; ran–*v*
1.030 Thom–*s*; offered–*v*; me–*i.o.*; piece–*d.o.*
1.031 neighbor; p.n.
1.032 strong; p.a.
1.033 girl; p.n.
1.034-1.035 Examples:
1.034 <u>Jerry</u> and <u>Jim</u> swam across the river.
1.035 Drew <u>jumped</u> in a boat and <u>rowed</u> across the river.
1.036 false
1.037 false
1.038 false
1.039 true

1.040 Example:
Knowing the basic parts of a sentence helps us to be sure we are using complete, correct sentences. If we understand where and how certain parts may be used, we can vary our sentence structure with more confidence.

1.041 It would not be complete because you would have no idea what the subject had done.

SECTION 2

2.1-2.5 Examples:

2.1 Betty and Sue were coming down the hill.

2.2 Frank and Tom and Sam played ball in the park.

2.3 Wandering down the road, I saw two squirrels in a tree.

2.4 Sharon is coming to my house tomorrow.

2.5 Sheltie puppies and calico kittens are my favorite animals.

2.6 fragment

2.7 Example:
putting together two or more complete thoughts linked by *and's*, *but's*, and *so's* as one sentence

2.8 Example:
It confuses the reader and makes the material harder to understand.

2.9 My father is an important man. He works all week so that I can eat, have clothes to wear, and a place to sleep. He repairs anything that breaks down around the house. He plays ball and builds things with me. He is my friend.

2.10 Examples:
a. My dog stays in our backyard. (S–V)
b. Her name is Sheba. (S–LV–PN)
c. She is gentle and friendly. (S–LV–PA)
d. She loves ice cream and other things I eat. (S–V–DO)
e. My friends bring her bones and toys. (S–V–IO–DO)

2.11 Yes, it is important. Otherwise we would turn in work with mistakes in it and this would lower our grade or make a bad impression.

2.12 Mr. Jones came over Sunday. He stayed for six hours, and I thought he would never go home. Finally, it was time to go to church. We asked him to go with us. He said he'd like to! After church he talked to Dad about the message and then believed in Jesus Christ as his Savior. Boy! Am I glad he didn't go home.

2.13-2.16 Examples:

2.13 Bitter was the lemon that was served with my tea.

2.14 Through the trees, dropping branches everywhere, ripped the wind.

2.15 Greener is the grass on the other side.

2.16 Through the crowd and into the street fought Randy.

2.17 Is Christy the daughter of the man who owns the garage?

2.18 After Mrs. James christened it, the ship slid down the ramps into the sea.

2.19 I saw the building as I was running down the street.

2.20 My father died when I was ten years old.

2.21 a. a wave of water that is icy
b. a weather front that brings cold air

2.22 a. a beautiful day
b. a day at a fair

2.23 a. a nice box
b. a box for collecting fines

2.24 a. a means of measuring weight —
According to this scale, you weigh 120 pounds.
b. a part of a fish —
The scales of the fish flashed in the sun as he jumped from the water.

2.25 a. forbidding —
His stern features frightened the children away.
b. part of a boat —
Go to the stern, McLain.

2.26 a. mail —
Would you post this letter for me on your way to work?
b. a wooden stick —
The fence posts barely showed above the newly fallen snow.

2.27 a. twenty-five cents —
Dorrie, would you lend me a quarter?
b. one-fourth —
Only a quarter of the class was present.

2.28 synonym

2.29 antonym

2.30 antonym

2.31 antonym

2.32 synonym

2.33-2.35 Examples:

2.33 rough, raspy, stiff, grainy, granular, abrasive, gritty, scratchy

2.34 holler, yell, whisper, scream, sob, shout, sputter, blabber, screech, stammer

2.35 magnificent, lovely, huge, isolated, elegant, frightening, spooky, scary, haunted, deserted, vacant, majestic

2.36 e

2.37 d

2.38 c

2.39 g

2.40 i

2.41 a

2.42 f

2.43-2.48 Examples:

2.43 conceal

2.44 throng, group

2.45 completed, ended

2.46 construct, make

2.47 reply

2.48 relate, disclose

2.49 Teacher check

2.50 Teacher check

2.51 fantastic, rewarding, etc.

2.52 trusting, warm, good natured, etc.

2.53 tasty, delicious, etc.

2.54 destructive, terrifying, etc.

2.55 exciting, informative, etc.

2.56 sweet, fragrant, etc.

2.57 delicious, yummy, etc.

2.58 strong, nauseating, etc.

2.59-2.63 Examples:

2.59 chalkboard – cool, smooth

2.60 wooden fence – rough, splintery

2.61 book – hard, smooth

2.62 rug – stubbly, rough, soft

2.63 car bumper – cold, rounded, smooth

2.64 a. contribute
b. construct
c. succeed
d. inform
e. denote

2.65 Examples:
nation, gnat, I, in, mint, gait, ton, at, mat, not, man, gain, tin, to, ion, an, tan, atom, on, it, aim (ing), again

2.66 Any order:
a. frag-ment
b. proof-read
c. am-bi-gu-i-ty
d. syn-o-nym
e. an-to-nym
f. con-no-ta-tion
g. de-no-ta-tion
h. viv-id
i. de-scrip-tive
j. con-cise
k. ac-cur-ate
l. ap-pre-ci-ate
m. suc-cess-ful
n. va-ri-e-ty
o. cre-a-tiv-i-ty
p. ac-com-mo-date
q. im-pre-sion
r. the-sau-rus
s. fa-vor-a-ble
t. ex-per-i-ence
u. in-for-ma-tion
v. con-tri-bu-tion
w. i-mag-i-na-tion
x. re-al-i-ty
y. con-struc-tive

SELF TEST 2

2.01 only part of a sentence, written as a whole sentence

2.02 a run-on sentence

2.03 to look over your work carefully, checking spelling, punctuation, and form

2.04 e

2.05 f

2.06 a

2.07 c

2.08 d

2.09-2.010 Examples:

2.09 Don and Ron went to the ballgame together.

2.010 Shelly turned over and got out of bed.

2.011 <u>flowers</u> <u>bloomed</u>

2.012 <u>father</u> <u>built</u>

2.013 <u>you</u>, <u>Do</u>, <u>know</u>

2.014 As she was sitting by the river, Melinda painted the picture.

2.015 When I was eight years old, my mother had my baby brother.

2.016 I saw three cars as I was walking down the lane.

2.017 It would not be complete because it would not tell whom or what the sentence is about.

2.018 Mr. Green–*s*; gave–*v*; Bobby–*i.o.*; rod–*d.o.*

2.019 Janey–*s*; wanted –*v*; doll–*d.o.*

2.020 Sally–*s*; offered–*v*; me–*i.o.*; piece–*d.o.*

2.021 Grandma–*s*; made–*v*; me–*i.o.*; dress–*d.o.*

2.022 Shirley–*s*; threw–*v*; ball–*d.o.*

2.023 Paul–*s*; gave–*v*; Susan–*i.o.*; turn–*d.o.*

2.024 f

2.025 e

2.026 a

2.027 h

2.028 c

2.029 g

2.030 b

2.031-2.035 Examples:

2.031 His <u>contribution</u> was appreciated.

2.032 John will <u>proofread</u> his work.

2.033 Some <u>information</u> is knowledge.

2.034 My first <u>impression</u> is favorable.

2.035 John gave Jane the <u>thesaurus</u>.

2.036 Mrs. Turner gave my mom her favorite recipe.

2.037 Did you see Nathan yesterday?

2.038 I went to Dallas Saturday.

2.039 On Sunday, Sherry wandered over to the fairgrounds.

2.040 b

2.041 e

2.042 a

2.043 d

2.044 f

SECTION 3

3.1 a.   con´ vict — noun
     convict —
    b.   con vict´ — verb

    c.   pro´ gress — noun
     progress —
    d.   pro gress´ — verb

    e.   pro´ duce — noun
     produce —
    f.   pro duce´ — verb

3.2 c

3.3 d

3.4 a

3.5 e

3.6 a. syl´ la ble
    b. ma ter´ i al
    c. com´ pan y
    d. tel´ e phone

3.7 Tom^{my}, come carry out the garbage.

3.8 Tom$_{my}$, come carry out the garbage.

3.9-3.12 Examples:

3.9 Will you come to my house?

3.10 Do you have your homework done?

3.11 I went to the store last night.

3.12 I got up late this morning.
    — Teacher check (3.9-3.12)

3.13 Come here!
    Mum ^{mum}!

3.14 Are you my friend?
    Mum ^{mum} mum mum?

3.15 Give me your pencil.
    Mum $_{mum\ mum\ mum}$.

3.16 Look out!
    Mum ^{mum}!

3.17-3.22 Examples:

3.17 a. Did you call me?
    b. I'm here.

3.18 a. I agree.
    b. I am relieved.

3.19 a. Did that really happen?
    b. Did she really do that?

3.20 a. I can't believe you said that.
    b. You are impossible!

3.21 a. I have to do that now?
    b. Do you want me now?

3.22 a. Come immediately.
    b. I have to do it now.

3.23 Examples:
    a. Shelly gave me her kitten.
    b. Sherman jumped over six feet!

3.24 Any order:
    a. to ask a question
    b. to end a sentence
    c. to give extra meaning to what we say
    d. to show emotion
    e. to show whether we are using a noun or verb
    f. to make the meaning of a sentence clear
    g. to add variety to our speaking and/or conversations

3.25-3.27 Examples:

3.25 a. you will receive an F in English.
    b. you will have to write an extra one.

3.26 a. we will play with my new game.
    b. you had better be on your best behavior.

3.27 a. be telling the truth.
    b. have the best grade in class.

3.28-3.30 Examples:

3.28 Amber—are you finished with the dishes?

3.29 Johnny—take out the garbage.

3.30 Kristin—feed the dog.

3.31 a break
    or brief time of waiting when speaking

3.32 a   emphasis
    b. meaning

3.33 attention

3.34 it is the important part—the part we don't want anyone to miss.

3.35 Mrs. Tandy is an excellent cook. She bakes homemade bread every week. The aroma drifts from her kitchen and into my bedroom window. I always go to see her when I smell that delicious aroma. She gives me some bread to eat while I visit with her.

3.36 b *or* d

3.37 e

3.38 c

3.39 a

3.40 artist; that

3.41 friend; he

3.42 student; moreover

3.43 furious; his

3.44 numbers: eight

3.45 tenses: past

3.46 things: newspapers

3.47-3.48 Either order:

3.47 no change

3.48 Sandra, put the dishes away.

3.49-3.50 Either order:

3.49 Mrs. Cortez, our neighbor is from Mexico.

3.50 Mrs. Cortez, our neighbor, is from Mexico.

3.51 Examples:
   a. Edith, what are you doing?
   b. What are you doing, Edith?
   c. What, Edith, are you doing?

3.52 Any order; any four:
   a. comma
   b. period / dash
   c. semi-colon / question mark
   d. colon / exclamation point

3.53-3.56

3.53 As the sun went down, beautiful colors filled the sky.

3.54 Behind the green house, three boys were playing ball.

3.55 He went into the store, while I waited outside.

3.56 After the bell rang, I went to the gym.

3.57 The last person usually hears something different from what was first said.

3.58 Hint:
Usually the sentences will be different because each person did not listen carefully and repeat exactly what was heard.

3.59 They are important because they help us understand what we read and say; they let us know when we have reached the end of a phrase or sentence.

3.60 statement

3.61 declarative

3.62 conversation

3.63 syllable

3.64 ridiculous

3.65 pronunciation

3.66 instruction

3.67 emphasis

3.68 gesture

3.69 signal

3.70 imperative

3.71 inflection

3.72 accent

3.73 pitch

3.74 important

3.75 dependent

3.76 punctuation

3.77 wait

3.78 hard

3.79 different

3.80 talk

3.81 silly

3.82 essential

3.83 fact

SELF TEST 3

3.01 b

3.02 g

3.03 o

3.04 e

3.05 f

3.06 p

3.07 a

3.08 h

3.09 s

3.010 c

3.011 i

3.012 k

3.013 d

3.014 j

3.015 t

3.016 q

3.017 m

3.018 n

3.019 l

3.020 It helps you catch mistakes before the teacher sees them.

3.021-3.022 Either order:

3.021 Mr. Dean, our friend went home.

3.022 Mr. Dean, our friend, went home.

3.023-3.025

3.023 After my class, I went to the grocery store.

3.024 When she got her report card, she burst into tears.

3.025 He played the piano, while I played the trumpet.

3.026 They are essential in understanding what is being read or said. They signal the end of a phrase or sentence.

3.027-3.031 Examples:

3.027 Nancy jumped into the swimming pool.

3.028 The dog grabbed the bone and ran.

3.029 Don is the second doctor in our family.

3.030 The car was blue with a white roof.

3.031 Jamie offered me part of her cherry tart.

3.032 Any four of the following:
a. semicolon
b. colon
c. comma
d. period
or question, exclamation, dash

3.033 Examples:
a. talk
b. wait
c. essential
d. stress

3.034 Examples:
a. question
b. serious
c. silence
d. easy

3.035 Any order:
a. to ask a question
b. to end a sentence
c. to show emotion
d. to show whether we are using a verb or noun
e. to make the meaning of a sentence clear
or to add variety to our speaking and/or conversation

LIFEPAC TEST

1. k
2. h
3. f
4. d
5. a
6. g
7. i
8. c
9. b
10. j
11. a. subject
    b. predicate
12. only part of a sentence, written as a whole sentence
13. to look over your work carefully, checking spelling, punctuation, and form
14. a. emphasis
    b. meaning
15. inflection
16. Simpson–*s*; gave–*v*; Jim–*i.o.*; B–*d.o.*
17. He–*s*; is–*v*; teacher–*p.n.*
18. Grandma–*s*; baked–*v*; pie–*d.o.*
19. She–*s*; is–*v*; lovely–*p.a.*
20. Leroy–*s*; swims–*v*
21.-25. Examples:
21. Dan sang. (S–V)
22. The quotation is descriptive. (S–LV–PA)
23. This book is a thesaurus. (S–LV–PN)
24. Shelly introduced her friend. (S–V–DO)
25. Our teacher gave us a vocabulary assignment. (S–V–IO–DO)
26. Any order; any three:
    a. to ask a question
    b. to end a sentence
    c. to show emotion
    or to make the meaning of a sentence clear, to add variety to our speaking and/or conversation, to show whether we are using a verb or noun
27. Any order; any three:
    a. colon
    b. comma/dot
    c. semicolon/dash
28. They are essential in understanding what is being read or said. They signal the end of a phrase or sentence.
29. b. adjective
30. b. offer
31. c. a word with a similar meaning
32. b. ambiguity
33. a. exclamatory
34. c. wait

ALTERNATE LIFEPAC TEST

1. k
2. h
3. b
4. i
5. d
6. a
7. e
8. f
9. j
10. g
11. follows a linking verb and renames the subject
12. indirect object
13. connotation
14. synonyms
15. a break or brief time of waiting when speaking
16. attention
17.   *s*   *v*   *i.o.*   *d.o.*
    Grandpa gave Dennis a new baseball
18.   *s*   *v*   *p.n.*
    Shirley is a good friend.
19.   *s*   *v*   *d.o.*
    Terry made a beautiful birdhouse.
20.   *s*   *v*   *p.a.*
    The rose was beautiful.
21.   *s*   *v*
    Roy ate at my house last Sunday.
22.-26. Examples:
22. *Ambiguity* causes confusion.
23. The *subject* of a sentence is essential.
24. Sherry made me a *ridiculous* hat for my birthday.
25. The cat was smiling above the description of the cat food.
26. *Punctuation* is essential.
27. c
28. d
29. a
30. Example:
    to get someone's attention or to show that something is very important and should be noticed
31. Any order:
    a. the end of a sentence or phrase (punctuation)
    b. calling attention to someone
    c. emphasizing a certain part of a sentence
32. a. con ver sa´ tion
    b. punc tu a´ tion
    c. de scrip´ tion

SPELLING TEST

1	noun	The subject of a sentence is a **noun**.	noun
2	subject	The **subject** of that sentence is house.	subject
3	predicate	The verb of the sentence is the **predicate**.	predicate
4	compound	Milli had a **compound** fracture of the leg.	compound
5	transitive	A **transitive** verb is an action word.	transitive
6	linking verb	The word "be" is a **linking verb**.	linking verb
7	adverb	An **adverb** often ends in "-ly".	adverb
8	introduce	Please **introduce** me to your friend.	introduce
9	vocabulary	Betty studied her **vocabulary** words.	vocabulary
10	important	Obeying your parents is **important**.	important
11	modify	The dress designer wanted to **modify** the style.	modify
12	adjective	An **adjective** answers the question "what kind of".	adjective
13	predicate adjective	A **predicate adjective** is a word that follows a linking verb and describes the subject.	predicate adjective
14	proofread	You should **proofread** your papers before you turn them in.	proofread
15	synonym	"Friendly" is a **synonym** of genial.	synonym
16	connotation	The **connotation** in her sentence was that I would have to work this weekend.	connotation
17	vivid	Henry gave the officer a **vivid** description of the accident.	vivid
18	concise	The statement was **concise**.	concise
19	appreciate	I really **appreciate** your offer.	appreciate
20	variety	**Variety** is the spice of life.	variety
21	creativity	Painting is an expression of **creativity**.	creativity
22	impression	My first **impression** was that he was a funny man.	impression
23	thesaurus	Charlie used a **thesaurus** to find a synonym.	thesaurus
24	experience	Going to the state fair was a wonderful **experience**.	experience
25	contribution	The Wright brothers made an important **contribution** to aviation.	contribution
26	reality	Sin in the world is a **reality**.	reality
27	pitch	Reggie Jackson struck out on that **pitch**.	pitch

SPELLING TEST

28	inflection	The **inflection** of her voice made it difficult to understand her.	inflection
29	pause	The singer had to **pause** between songs.	pause
30	imperative	It is **imperative** that I see you tonight.	imperative
31	exclamatory	An **exclamatory** sentence shows surprise or shock.	exclamatory
32	dependent	Billy is **dependent** on his parents.	dependent
33	semicolon	A **semicolon** is a punctuation mark.	semicolon
34	punctuation	Be sure to use **punctuation**.	punctuation
35	ridiculous	Some types of humor are **ridiculous**.	ridiculous
36	statement	Henry made the **statement** that he was hungry.	statement
37	communicate	Today we can **communicate** via satellite.	communicate
38	instruction	Follow each **instruction**.	instruction
39	quotation	"Pray without ceasing" is a **quotation**.	quotation
40	conversation	I had a **conversation** with Mr. Bidle.	conversation

LANGUAGE ARTS 704

ALTERNATE LIFEPAC TEST

NAME _____

DATE _____

SCORE _____

82
102

Match these items with the definition (each answer, 2 points).

1. _____ indirect object

2. _____ antonym

3. _____ predicate adjective

4. _____ exclamatory

5. _____ linking verb

6. _____ sentence

7. _____ interrogative

8. _____ denotation

9. _____ subject

10. _____ pitch

a. expresses a complete thought

b. follows a linking verb

c. word with a similar meaning

d. an intransitive verb that links the subject with another word

e. sentence that asks a question

f. dictionary meaning of a word

g. tone of the voice in speech

h. word with an opposite meaning

i. sentence that shows strong emotion

j. who or what the sentence is about

k. noun that indicates to or for whom or for what the subject acts

Complete these sentences (each answer, 3 points).

11. A predicate nominative _____

_____ .

12. The word that comes between the verb and the direct object is the _____

_____ .

13. The emotional overtones of a word are called _____ .

14. Words with similar meanings are called _____ .

15. The pause is _____

_____ .

16. A pause can be used to call _____ .

Label the parts of speech. In the following sentences write *s* over the subject, *v* over the verb, *i.o.* over the indirect object, *d.o.* over the direct object, *p.n.* over the predicate nominative, and *p.a.* over the predicate adjective (each answer, 1 point).

17. Grandpa gave Dennis a new baseball.

18. Shirley is a good friend.

19. Terry made a beautiful birdhouse.

20. The rose was beautiful.

21. Roy ate at my house last Sunday.

Use five of your spelling words each in a sentence. Use a different sentence pattern for each answer (each answer, 4 points).

22. _____

_____

23. _____

_____

24. _____

_____

25. _____

_____

26. _____

_____

Match the word with its synonym (each answer, 2 points).

27. _____ disregard

28. _____ involve

29. _____ affect

a. influence

b. frighten

c. ignore

d. entangle

Answer this question (this answer, 5 points).

30. Why would we want to call attention to or emphasize a certain part of a sentence?

_____

_____

_____

_____

Complete these activities (each answer, 3 points).

31. List three things that a pause indicates when we are speaking.

a. _____

b. _____

c. _____

32. Divide these words into syllables. Put an accent mark on the syllable that should be stressed.

a. conversation _____

b. punctuation _____

c. descriptive _____

ALTERNATE SPELLING TEST

1	sentence	Good **sentence** structure is important.	sentence
2	verb	The **verb** is the action in a sentence.	verb
3	inverted	Joey **inverted** his glass, dumping the contents all over the table.	inverted
4	direct object	The **direct object** usually follows the predicate.	direct object
5	intransitive	**Intransitive** verbs do not receive a direct object.	intransitive
6	indirect object	The **indirect object** usually precedes the direct object.	indirect object
7	punctuation	Be sure to use correct **punctuation** at the end of each sentence.	punctuation
8	pronounce	Learn to **pronounce** each word correctly.	pronounce
9	vocabulary	Betty studied her **vocabulary** words.	vocabulary
10	structure	A dam is a **structure** for holding back water.	structure
11	important	Obeying your parents is **important**.	important
12	identify	John could not **identify** the thief that stole is wallet.	identify
13	preposition	The word "of" is a **preposition**.	preposition
14	predicate nominative	A **predicate nominative** is a noun or pronoun that follows a linking verb.	predicate nominative
15	predicate adjective	A **predicate adjective** is a word that follows a linking verb and describes the subject.	predicate adjective
16	fragment	Jane picked up each **fragment** of the broken glass.	fragment
17	ambiguity	**Ambiguity** means there may be more than one meaning.	ambiguity
18	antonym	"Hot" is an **antonym** of cold.	antonym
19	denotation	**Denotation** is the exact meaning of a sentence.	denotation
20	descriptive	Teri's paper about Rome was very **descriptive**.	descriptive
21	accurate	Steve gave an **accurate** description of the lost boy.	accurate
22	appreciate	I really **appreciate** your offer.	appreciate
23	successful	The businessman was very **successful**.	successful
24	accommodate	The room was not large enough to **accommodate** all seventy students.	accommodate
25	favorable	My review of her work was **favorable**.	favorable
26	information	Her **information** was not valid.	information

ALTERNATE SPELLING TEST

27	imagination	Her **imagination** ran wild.	imagination
28	constructive	**Constructive** criticism is difficult to accept.	constructive
29	accent	Kate spoke with a Swedish **accent**.	accent
30	pronunciation	Be sure to use correct **pronunciation**.	pronunciation
31	declarative	A statement is a **declarative** sentence.	declarative
32	interrogative	A question is an **interrogative** sentence.	interrogative
33	difficult	Some math problems are **difficult** to understand.	difficult
34	important	Respecting your elders is **important**.	important
35	syllable	The word bug has only one **syllable**.	syllable
36	emphasis	Paul placed much **emphasis** on serving God.	emphasis
37	statement	Henry made the **statement** that he was hungry.	statement
38	gesture	He made a **gesture** with his hands.	gesture
39	separate	The teacher wanted to **separate** the boys from the girls.	separate
40	signal	At the **signal** you should steal second base.	signal

LANGUAGE ARTS 705

Unit 5: The Nature of English

TEACHER NOTES

MATERIALS NEEDED FOR LIFEPAC	
Required	**Suggested**
None	None

ADDITIONAL LEARNING ACTIVITIES

Section 1: The Nature of Language

1. Choose an activity, recipe, or other item requiring directions. Have the students list each signal word as you read the directions.

2. Devise a game and work out the directions for it. Play the game to see if the directions can be followed easily.

3. Choose a Psalm to read. Write all the words you find for feelings.

4. Write down all the words for signals you see on your way to school or downtown. Do you see any signal words at school?

Section 2: The Structure of English

1. Read samples of informal, formal, and nonstandard English aloud and let the students distinguish among them.

2. Take a paragraph or two of formal English from a selection such as The Declaration of Independence. Read it and rewrite it in informal English. Do not use nonstandard English.

3. Find examples of written formal, informal, and nonstandard English. Advertisements often contain nonstandard English.

Section 3: The Correct Usage of English

1. Conjugate the present and past tenses of a regular verb on the board as a model. Give the students another regular verb to conjugate.

	Present	Past
	Singular	
first person—I	jump	jumped
second person—you	jump	jumped
third person—he, she, it	jumps	jumped
	Plural	
first person—we	jump	jumped
second person—you	jump	jumped
third person—they	jump	jumped

Point out the -s form used in the third person singular present tense.

2. Play "verb baseball."
   Make up some sentences using the often confused verbs *lie* and *lay*, *raise* and *rise*, and *sit* and *set*. Some sentences should be incorrect. Read them one by one to another group. A member of the second group must identify the sentences as right or wrong within ten seconds or be out. When a team misses three sentences in a row, it strikes out and the other side is "up at bat." The first team that is ahead after three complete innings wins.

3. Look up the principle parts of some irregular verbs (blow, eat, write, be, being, and so on) in a dictionary. Write a conjugation of three of them in the present and past tenses.

4. Look at some lines in the King James Version of the Bible. Do you see any unusual verb forms? Write any examples of these forms.

5. Handout Bible Puzzle Work Sheet.

Administer the LIFEPAC Spelling Test.
The test is provided in this Teacher's Guide.
Evaluate the tests and review the words the students spelled incorrectly.
If necessary, review all of the words in the unit to prepare for the alternate spelling test.
Administer the Alternate LIFEPAC Spelling test that is provided in this Teacher's Guide.

Administer the LIFEPAC Test.
The test is to be administered in one session. Give no help except with directions.
Evaluate the tests and review areas where the students have done poorly.
Review the pages and activities that stress the concepts tested.
If necessary, administer the Alternate LIFEPAC Test.

» ADDITIONAL ACTIVITY ANSWER KEY

Bible puzzle: I AM THE ALPHA AND OMEGA, THE BEGINNING AND THE END.

   a. panda
   b. me
   c. I
   d. them
   e. nine
   f. that
   g. begin
   h. had
   i. hang
   j. lead
   k. gone

The additional activity on the following page may be reproduced as a student worksheet.

» ADDITIONAL ACTIVITY

Bible Puzzle Worksheet

```
__  __ __   __ __ __    __ __ __ __ __    __ __ __    __ __ __ __ __ ,
1   2  3    4  5  6     7  8  9  10 11    12 13 14    15 16 17 18 19
```

```
__ __ __   __ __ __ __ __ __ __ __    __ __ __    __ __ __    __ __ __ .
20 21 22   23 24 25 26 27 28 29 30 31  32 33 34    35 36 37   38 39 40
```

a. a black and white bear from China

          __ __ __ __ __
          9 2 13 14 11

b. objective case of *I*

          __ __
          3 6

c. nominative case of *me*

          __
          1

d. objective case of *they*

          __ __ __ __
          4 5 17 16

e. the number after eight

          __ __ __ __
          27 26 33 22

f. this and _____

          __ __ __ __
          20 21 19 35

g. present tense of *began*

          __ __ __ __ __
          23 37 25 29 28

h. past tense of *have*

          __ __ __
          36 12 34

i. present tense of *hanged*

          __ __ __ __
          10 7 30 31

j. present tense of *led*

          __ __ __ __
          8 24 32 40

k. past participle of *go*

          __ __ __ __
          18 15 39 38

(Revelation 21:6)

ANSWER KEYS

SECTION 1

1.1   Wait
1.2   Go
1.3   Danger
1.4   Turn Left
1.5   Throw
1.6   lend
1.7   put, get
1.8   begin
1.9   exit
1.10   entrance
1.11   Step-by-step check list activity
1.12
1. write
2. fold, give
3. ask, write, larger
4. below, write, backward
5. subtract, smaller
6. below, write, backward
7. add
8. after, ask, read

1.13   Teacher check
1.14-1.23 Examples:
1.14   happiness
1.15   fear
1.16   pain
1.17   anger
1.18   love
1.19   fear
1.20   love
1.21   happiness
1.22   pain
1.23   anger
1.24
  a. affection
  b. romance
  c. devotion
1.25
  a. ache
  b. misery
  c. agony
1.26
  a. joy
  b. delight
  c. contentment
1.27
  a. fright
  b. scared
  c. horror
1.28
  a. remorse
  b. guilt
  c. shame
1.29
  a. weary
  b. fatigued
  c. exhausted

1.30
  a. tranquility
  b. calm
  c. harmony
1.31
  a. uncomfortable
  b. self-conscious
  c. embarrassed
1.32
  a. courage
  b. valor
  c. heroism
1.33
  a. rage
  b. displeasure
  c. resentment
1.34   Teacher check
1.35-1.59 Sentences will vary.
      Examples:
1.35   I'm not finished *yet*.
1.36   Don't *yell* in the lunch room.
1.37   She knit the socks with *yarn*.
1.38   It rained *yesterday*.
1.39   *My* feet are cold.
1.40   I like to *type* letters.
1.41   *Try* to finish your homework.
1.42   The *spry* old man was jogging.
1.43   They *badly* needed a new roof.
1.44   She was *very* pretty.
1.45   He had *many* friends.
1.46   The *mystery* of the missing book was solved.
1.47   The cross is a Christian *symbol*.
1.48   The tin can is a *cylinder*.
1.49   The *gypsy* lived in a wagon.
1.50   The *youth* was tall and thin.
1.51   We went *through* the old part of town.
1.52   Prayer is good for the *soul*.
1.53   He is a *poultry* farmer.
1.54   His *shoulder* was broken in the game.
1.55   The road was *rough*.
1.56   The meat was *tough*.
1.57   The *cloud* appeared at the end of the game.
1.58   I bought a *pound* of butter.
1.59   He hit a *foul* ball.
      — Teacher check

SELF TEST 1

1.01 false
1.02 true
1.03 false
1.04 true
1.05 false
1.06 true
1.07 true
1.08 true
1.09 false
1.010 true
1.011 danger
1.012 turn
1.013 exit
1.014 come
1.015 do
1.016 tired
1.017 anger
1.018 fear
1.019 agony
1.020 uncomfortable
1.021 category
1.022 language
1.023 feelings
1.024 commands
  or directions
1.025 directions
  or commands
1.026 communication
  or communicating
1.027 Examples:
  a. lettuce
  b. carrots
  c. celery
1.028 Examples:
  a. come
  b. go
  c. stop
1.029 Examples:
  a. language
  b. ability to learn
  c. ability to use language

SECTION 2

2.1 approximately
2.2 anywhere
2.3 finished
2.4 dived
2.5 believe
2.6 odd
2.7 dismissed
2.8 almost
2.9 fail
2.10 victory
2.11 try to
2.12 once
2.13 repair
2.14 that
2.15 from
2.16 traded
2.17 betray
2.18 defend
2.19-2.26 Sentences will vary.
  Examples:
2.19 You may go *anywhere* you wish.
2.20 Are you *finished* with your work?
2.21 I *believe* you are ready to eat lunch.
2.22 He *failed* his history class.
2.23 Did you get that *from* Harry?
2.24 She likes to *trade* miniature dolls for her collection.
2.25 How many *victories* does your team have?
2.26 Bill's hobby is *repairing* broken bicycles.
2.27 After high school, many students continue their education and attend college.
2.28 I am in school now.
2.29 He will end his sermon by reading a passage from the Bible.
2.30 Because I failed my last test, I need to study to raise my grade in history.
2.31 I like ice cream as well as frozen yogurt bars.
2.32 If the team wins the championship, we will have a celebration.
2.33 Since Danny skipped the second grade, he is the youngest member of our class.
2.34 Soon we will visit near Houston, Texas.
2.35 For a tall girl her feet are small.
2.36 They were joined in Holy Matrimony.
2.37 Mary gave us a warning that she was going to set a record for twiddling her thumbs.
2.38 Except for Tom and two others, we all enjoyed the concert.
  or
  All of us except Tom and two others enjoyed the concert.

SELF TEST 2

2.39 I am not going to play softball until next Wednesday.

2.40 <u>about</u>; approximately

2.41 <u>if and when</u>; if (or) when

2.42 <u>Due to</u>; Because of

2.43 <u>expect</u>; suppose (believe)

2.44 <u>due to the fact that</u>; because

2.45 <u>done</u>; finished

2.46 <u>used to have</u>; once had

2.47 <u>expect</u>; believe

2.48 <u>anyplace</u>; anywhere

2.49 <u>by means of</u>; by

2.50 <u>try and</u>; try to

2.51 <u>off of</u>; from

2.52-2.81 Sentences will vary. Examples:

2.52 The *pedal* of the bicycle fell off.

2.53 The flower *petal* was pretty.

2.54 The man will *peddle* all the goods.

2.55 I like to *write* letters to my friend.

2.56 The answers are *right*.

2.57 The *rite* will start at two o'clock.

2.58 The golfer yelled, "*Fore!*"

2.59 I saw *four* rabbits in the field.

2.60 I voted *for* him.

2.61 The *rain* fell all night.

2.62 The *rein* on the horse broke.

2.63 The king will *reign* for many years.

2.64 I bought a *pair* of shoes.

2.65 I can *pare* the apple.

2.66 I ate the *pear*.

2.67 The *road* is rough.

2.68 We *rode* on the train.

2.69 He *rowed* the boat.

2.70 I like to *sew* new clothes.

2.71 The farmer will *sow* the seeds.

2.72 The building is *so* tall.

2.73 The dog smelled the man's *scent*.

2.74 I *sent* the letter.

2.75 I need one more *cent*.

2.76 I live over *there*.

2.77 *Their* dog won the prize.

2.78 *They're* going to the game.

2.79 The usher helped us down the *aisle*.

2.80 The beach was on the west side of the *isle*.

2.81 *I'll* fix the broken vase.
— Teacher check

2.01 true

2.02 false

2.03 true

2.04 false

2.05 false

2.06 <u>F</u>

2.07 <u>S</u>

2.08 <u>F</u>

2.09 <u>F</u>

2.010 <u>S</u>

2.011 <u>S</u>

2.012 <u>F</u>

2.013 <u>S</u>

2.014 <u>F</u>

2.015 <u>S</u>

2.016 d

2.017 f

2.018 i

2.019 j

2.020 h

2.021 c

2.022 a

2.023 g

2.024 b

2.025 e

2.026 Almost

2.027 believe

2.028 odd

2.029 from

2.030 victories

2.031 at this time

2.032 by means
or by means of

2.033 due to the fact that

2.034 in the near future

2.035 with the result

2.036 a. now
b. by
c. because
d. soon
e. therefore
or <u>Since</u> I did not study...

2.037 communicate—to give information by speaking and/or writing

2.038 category—a group or division in general system of classification

2.039 colloquial—informal and casual speech

2.040 idiom—a phrase or expression whose meaning cannot be understood from the ordinary meanings of the words in it

2.041 cliché—a worn out idea or trite expression

SECTION 3

3.1 loves
3.2 are going
3.3 sing, play
3.4 runs, jumps
3.5 play
3.6 plays
3.7 will leave, stay, return
3.8 should try
3.9 live
3.10 lives
3.11 Bob
3.12 boys
3.13 Mary, Diane
3.14 Scott, Richie, Mark
3.15 team
3.16 birds
3.17 bird
3.18 bird, squirrel
3.19 child
3.20 children

3.21	subject:	boys
	verb:	are
3.22	subject:	Jane
	verb:	is
3.23	subject:	he
	verb:	was
3.24	subject:	We
	verb:	were
3.25	subject:	Laurie, Greg
	verb:	are
3.26	subject:	Tom
	verb:	is
3.27	subject:	pioneers
	verb:	were
3.28	subject:	grandfather
	verb:	was
3.29	subject:	flowers
	verb:	are
3.30	subject:	few
	verb:	were
3.31	subject:	I
	verb:	do
3.32	subject:	He
	verb:	does
3.33	subject:	We
	verb:	do
3.34	subject:	family
	verb:	does
3.35	subject:	coach
	verb:	inspires

3.36	subject:	brother, sister
	verb:	read, paint
3.37	subject:	few
	verb:	seem
3.38	subject:	One
	verb:	knows
3.39	subject:	Mike, Bob
	verb:	deliver
3.40	subject:	You
	verb:	receive
3.41	subject:	knowledge, teachings
	verb:	help
3.42	subject:	family, I
	verb:	attend
3.43	subject:	stack
	verb:	weighs
3.44	subject:	lights
	verb:	blink
3.45	subject:	Each
	verb:	makes

3.46	ask	asked
	begin	began
	blow	blew
	break	broke
	bring	brought
	build	built
	catch	caught
	choose	chose
	climb	climbed
	do	did
	drink	drank
	eat	ate
	fight	fought
	fly	flew
	freeze	froze
	go	went
	hit	hit
	know	knew
	learn	learned
	let	let
	put	put
	ring	rang
	set	set
	speak	spoke
	take	took
	throw	threw
	trip	tripped
	try	tried
	wish	wished
	write	wrote

3.47	~~tell~~	told
3.48	~~pushes~~	pushed
3.49	~~studies~~	studied
	~~turns~~	turned
	~~writes~~	wrote
3.50	~~go~~	went
	~~drink~~	drank
	~~play~~	played
	~~eat~~	ate
	~~build~~	built
	~~take~~	took
3.51	~~sewed~~	sews
	~~listened~~	listens
3.52	~~interrupt~~	interrupted
	~~feel~~	felt
	~~ask~~	asked
3.53	~~sing~~	sang
	~~tell~~	told
	~~sleep~~	slept
3.54	~~can~~	could
3.55	~~choose~~	will choose
	~~watched~~	watch
3.56	~~ran~~	run

3.57 Mary is eating (lunch).

3.58 The children play (games).

3.59 God answered our (prayers).

3.60 Bill told us the (truth).

3.61 Mark wrote a good book (report) for English.

3.62 My father and mother like my (sister) and (me).

3.63 Do you like (cheese)?

3.64 I will see (you) in the morning.

3.65 John watched (airplanes) at the airport all day yesterday.

3.66 I read the (Bible) every day.

3.67-3.76

	Correct verb	Direct object
3.67	lay	• keys
3.68	lie	
3.69	lying	
3.70	laying	• rug
3.71	laid	• towels
3.72	lay	
3.73	lying	
3.74	lay	• cups
3.75	lies	
3.76	laid	• baby

3.77-3.86

	Correct verb	Direct object
3.77	set	• packages
3.78	sit	
3.79	sitting	
3.80	setting	• couch
3.81	set	• laundry
3.82	sat	
3.83	sit	
3.84	sat; set	• lamp
3.85	sits	
3.86	settings	• cans

3.87-3.96

	Correct verb	Direct object
3.87	rise	
3.88	raise	• voice
3.89	rising	
3.90	raising	• temperature
3.91	rose	
3.92	raised	• horses
3.93	rises	
3.94	rose	
3.95	rise	
3.96	raised	• grade

3.97-3.131

	Correct verb	Direct object
3.97	Lie	
3.98	rise	
3.99	sit	
3.100	raise	• window
3.101	lay	• shoes
3.102	raised	• kite
3.103	rises	
3.104	laying	• foundation
3.105	sat	
3.106	lying	
3.107	set	• flowers
3.108	set	• flowers
3.109	raising	• children
3.110	rose	
3.111	sitting	
3.112	lie	
3.113	setting	• food
3.114	laid	• glove
3.115	lay	
3.116	Set	• thermostat
3.117	rise	
3.118	Laying	• books
3.119	rose	
3.120	sitting	
3.121	Raising	• chickens
3.122	Rising	
3.123	raised	• hand
3.124	raise	• flag
3.125	Lay	• blankets
3.126	lay	
3.127	sits	
3.128	set	• lamp
3.129	laid	• egg
3.130	sat	
3.131	lying	

3.132-3.141

	Subject	Object
3.132	I	
3.133		me
3.134		her
3.135	she	
3.136	he	
3.137		him
3.138	She	her
3.139	I	him; her
3.140	I	
3.141		me

3.142-3.151

	Subject	Object
3.142	we	
3.143		us
3.144		them
3.145	they	
3.146	Who	
3.147		whom
3.148	We	
3.149		us
3.150	they	
3.151		whom

3.152-3.161

	Incorrectly used pronoun	Correct pronoun
3.152	I	me
3.153	Us; he	We; him
3.154	him	he
3.155	Him; her	He; she
3.156	them	they
3.157	we	us
3.158	me	I
3.159	Whom; I	Who; me
3.160	me	I
3.161	Her; he	She; him

3.162 Teacher check

3.163-3.187 Sentences will vary.
Examples:

3.163 I was *annoyed* by his behavior.

3.164 He *blew* out the candles.

3.165 My father *bought* some cattle.

3.166 Lisa *brought* her cat home.

3.167 Joe *caught* fine catfish.

3.168 Jerry *climbed* the ladder quickly.

3.169 Kathy *drew* a beautiful bird.

3.170 My sister is *engaged* to be married.

3.171 The rooster *flew* to the fence.

3.172 His body *fought* off the infection.

3.173 The ice cream *froze* quickly.

3.174 He *guessed* what was in the box.

3.175 Grandmother *knew* you would come.

3.176 Timothy *learned* to read when he was four.

3.177 My parents have been *married* fifteen years.

3.178 Jack needs to *quit* chewing so much gum.

3.179 Carrie *received* an award in Sunday school.

3.180 He *rode* his pony proudly to the house.

3.181 She *scraped* the plates and washed them.

3.182 Columbus and his men *sought* a passage to India.

3.183 Mrs. Stevens *taught* Joe in the fourth grade.

3.184 Tommy *threw* the winning pass.

3.185 My mother *typed* the paper for me.

3.186 I *wrote* a poem about spring.

3.187 The little poodle *yielded* the bone to the great dane.

— Teacher check

SELF TEST 3

3.01	true	
3.02	false	
3.03	true	
3.04	false	
3.05	false	
3.06	true	
3.07	true	
3.08	false	
3.09	true	
3.010	true	
3.011	lie	
3.012	sitting	
3.013	raised	
3.014	we; are	
3.015	I	
3.016	me	
3.017	she; him; they	
3.018	Who; hit	
3.019	goes; us	
3.020	brought	
3.021	wait	
3.022	beware	
3.023	write	
3.024	delight	
3.025	courage	
3.026	guilt	
3.027	b	
3.028	a	
3.029	d	
3.030	c	
3.031	<u>at the conclusion of</u>	after
3.032	<u>if and when</u>	if/when
3.033	<u>in the vicinity of</u>	near
3.034	me	
3.035	you	
3.036	her	
3.037	us	
3.038	lay	
3.039	set	
3.040	raise	

LIFEPAC TEST

1. true
2. true
3. false
4. true
5. true
6. false
7. false
8. false
9. true
10. false
11. true
12. j
13. f
14. d
15. i
16. h
17. e
18. c
19. b
20. a
21. g
22. k
23. about
24. due to the fact that
25. with the result that
26. done
27. at the present time
28. approximately
29. because
30. so
31. finished
32. now
33. Set
34. Lay
35. rise
36. me
37. We
38. her

ALTERNATE LIFEPAC TEST

1. true
2. false
3. true
4. true
5. true
6. false
7. false
8. false
9. true
10. true
11. false
12. j
13. f
14. d
15. i
16. h
17. e
18. c
19. b
20. a
21. g
22. k
23. how come
24. at the conclusion of
25. about
26. done
27. at the present time
28. why
29. after
30. approximately
31. finished
32. now

SPELLING TEST

1	pedal	Larry tried to **pedal** his bicycle faster.	pedal
2	peddle	He tried to **peddle** his fruit to the grocery store.	peddle
3	write	He will be able to **write** great poetry someday.	write
4	rite	Our church is going to hold the **rite** of baptism next week.	rite
5	four	There are **four** new students in our classroom.	four
6	for	**For** Tom's birthday, they went roller skating.	for
7	rein	He held tightly to the horse's **rein**.	rein
8	pair	She just bought a new **pair** of shoes.	pair
9	pear	That **pear** was very tasty.	pear
10	rode	He **rode** the train to the next town.	rode
11	rowed	We **rowed** almost the entire day before we crossed the lake.	rowed
12	sow	I wonder what type of seeds he will **sow** this year.	sow
13	scent	The **scent** of the cherry blossoms was in the air.	scent
14	sent	Jesus was **sent** by God to save the world.	sent
15	there	**There** he is!	there
16	they're	**They're** going on a picnic today.	they're
17	isle	The **isle** of Patmos is where John was imprisoned.	isle
18	annoyed	The teacher was **annoyed** by the noise.	annoyed
19	bought	She **bought** a new coat.	bought
20	caught	Bill **caught** four trout in that stream.	caught
21	climbed	I **climbed** up ten flights of stairs to get to Sue's apartment.	climbed
22	engaged	Tom and Cindy are **engaged** to be married.	engaged
23	flew	The eagle **flew** higher and higher.	flew
24	fought	The United States **fought** Germany in World War II.	fought
25	guessed	She **guessed** that he was hiding something.	guessed
26	learned	She **learned** how to spell a new word yesterday.	learned
27	quit	Bob **quit** the team because of his sore leg.	quit

SPELLING TEST

28	road	The **road** was very smooth.	road
29	sought	They all **sought** a new job.	sought
30	taught	He **taught** them how to throw a football.	taught
31	typed	She **typed** ten pages of her report last night.	typed
32	yielded	Christ **yielded** His life for us.	yielded
33	yet	He is not **yet** finished with his work.	yet
34	yarn	The cat played with the ball of **yarn**.	yarn
35	my	**My** house is on the left.	my
36	try	I will **try** to get to school on time.	try
37	badly	He did **badly** on the test.	badly
38	many	**Many** people volunteered for the job.	many
39	mystery	It is a **mystery** how he escaped.	mystery
40	cylinder	This tin can is shaped like a **cylinder**.	cylinder
41	youth	The **youth** of America are important to its success as a nation.	youth
42	soul	Christ came to save everyone's **soul**.	soul
43	shoulder	His **shoulder** is very sore.	shoulder
44	tough	The meat is very **tough**.	tough
45	pound	These items weigh more than a **pound**.	pound

LANGUAGE ARTS 705

ALTERNATE LIFEPAC TEST

NAME _____

DATE _____

SCORE _____

50 / 63

Answer *true* **or** *false* (each answer, 1 point).

1. _____ Clichés and slang are seldom used when writing formal English.

2. _____ Regular verbs do not form their past tenses by ending with *-ed* or *-d*.

3. _____ You will seldom confuse which pronoun or verb to use if you understand subjects and objects.

4. _____ Following or giving directions would be difficult if we didn't have words for signals.

5. _____ *Redundant* means *extra*; *not needed*.

6. _____ When a personal pronoun is used as an object in a sentence, it is in the nominative case.

7. _____ The word *shame* is *not* a word for a feeling.

8. _____ Action verbs do *not* end with *-s* or *-es* when the subject is singular.

9. _____ The word *catch* is an irregular verb.

10. _____ Nonstandard English is illiterate.

11. _____ Words for signals and feelings are *not* word categories.

Match these items (each answer, 2 points).

12. _____ eat

13. _____ formal English

14. _____ lying, sitting, rising

15. _____ stop

16. _____ -ed or -d

17. _____ laying, setting, raising

18. _____ sorrow

19. _____ she, we, they, you

20. _____ -s or -es

21. _____ her, us, them, you

22. _____ informal English

a. a verb ending used to correctly form subject verb agreement

b. nominative case pronouns

c. a word for *feeling*

d. verbs that do not have objects

e. verbs that need objects

f. used for writing school assignments

g. objective case pronouns

h. a verb ending used to form the past tense of regular verbs

i. a word for a *signal*

j. an irregular verb

k. used for writing a note to friend

Read the following paragraph and find five redundant or informal expressions that are not appropriate when using formal English. Write these expressions in the space provided (each answer, 3 points).

When I was younger, I could not understand how come my parents read the Bible every single day of the week. My father told me he read a chapter a day. At the conclusion of one and a half years, he had read through the Bible in its entirety. Once finished, he would start back at the beginning. It took him about five minutes to read a chapter and another five minutes to meditate and absorb what he had read. He told me that it was the best ten minutes of the day. When he was done, he felt refreshed and at ease. At the present time, I spend ten minutes a day with the Bible, and it really is one of the best parts of my day.

23. _____

24. _____

25. _____

26. _____

27. _____

Rewrite the errors expressed in your answers for activities 23.- 27. by expressing the ideas clearly and in fewer words. Your answers should be correct for formal usage (each answer, 3 points).

28. _____

29. _____

30. _____

31. _____

32. _____

ALTERNATE SPELLING TEST

1	petal	The **petal** on the flower was beautiful.	petal
2	peddle	He tried to **peddle** his fruit to the grocery store.	peddle
3	right	I thought that I was **right**.	right
4	fore	Before he hit the golf ball, the golfer, shouted, "**Fore!**"	fore
5	rain	I hope it doesn't **rain** today.	rain
6	reign	The **reign** of the king was short.	reign
7	pair	She just bought a new **pair** of shoes.	pair
8	pare	Mother told me to **pare** the apple.	pare
9	road	To get to Mike's house, take the **road** on the left.	road
10	rode	He **rode** the train to the next town.	rode
11	sew	She learned how to **sew** from her mother.	sew
12	so	**So**, you are going to the game tonight.	so
13	scent	The **scent** of the cherry blossoms was in the air.	scent
14	cent	One penny is the same thing as one **cent**.	cent
15	there	**There** he is!	there
16	their	**Their** teacher is very strict.	their
17	they're	**They're** going on a picnic today.	they're
18	aisle	I had to walk down the **aisle** to get to the front of the church.	aisle
19	I'll	**I'll** see if I can help you.	I'll
20	blew	The wind **blew** very hard.	blew
21	brought	They **brought** their new puppy to our house.	brought
22	drew	He **drew** a beautiful picture of Sally.	drew
23	flew	The eagle **flew** higher and higher.	flew
24	froze	The water in the lake **froze** last night.	froze
25	knew	He **knew** that Fred was acting strangely.	knew
26	married	I have been **married** ten years now.	married
27	received	She **received** a new coat for Christmas.	received
28	scraped	We **scraped** the snow off the sidewalk.	scraped

ALTERNATE SPELLING TEST

29	threw	We **threw** away all the trash.	threw
30	wrote	Bill **wrote** to his parents.	wrote
31	yielded	Christ **yielded** His life for us.	yielded
32	yell	She said not to **yell**.	yell
33	yesterday	The sun shone brightly **yesterday**.	yesterday
34	type	That **type** of shirt is not warm enough.	type
35	spry	She had a very **spry** walk.	spry
36	very	He wants to go **very** much.	very
37	mystery	It is a **mystery** how he escaped.	mystery
38	symbol	The **symbol** for Christianity is the cross.	symbol
39	gypsy	The **gypsy** was dressed in ragged clothes.	gypsy
40	through	You can go to the store **through** the alley.	through
41	poultry	The grocery store has many **poultry** items.	poultry
42	rough	This road is very **rough**.	rough
43	cloud	There is not a **cloud** in the sky.	cloud
44	foul	After Dick had committed his fifth **foul**, he was taken out of the basketball game.	foul
45	my	**My** house is on the left.	my

LANGUAGE ARTS 706

Unit 6: The Mechanics of English

TEACHER NOTES

MATERIALS NEEDED FOR LIFEPAC	
Required	Suggested
None	• students may wish to refer to Language Arts LIFEPAC 703 and the biography they previously wrote • reference books or online sources

ADDITIONAL LEARNING ACTIVITIES

Language Arts LIFEPAC 706 is lengthy and students are asked to do a great deal of writing. It may be a challenge for some pupils to finish this LIFEPAC in three-and-a-half to four weeks. Additional learning activities may be used with students who work quickly and selected ones may help reinforce basic skills for slower students.

Section 1: Capitalization

1. Discussion questions:

    a. How do common nouns and proper nouns differ? (Proper nouns are capitalized and they are more specific.)

    b. When you study the rules of capitalization, what two things should you look for?

2. One group prepares a set of sentences needing capitalization. The other group has a set time (30 seconds per sentence or so) in which to make needed corrections. For any missed capitals the group must write the rule and two examples. After five sentences another group tries correcting sentences. The group making the fewest errors wins.

3. Find a copy of *Pilgrim's Progress* or the works of some of the early American and English writers. Notice the use of capitalization. Does it conform to today's standards?

Section 2: Inside Punctuation

1. Discussion questions:

    a. In what ways does punctuation add meaning to sentences? (It gives clarity and emphasis.)

    b. How do we punctuate a date in the middle of a sentence? (Use a comma after the day and year: On June 3, 1974, my father was born.)

    c. How do we punctuate a city and state in the middle of a sentence? (Place a comma after the city and the state: In San Diego, California, a wonderful zoo draws many visitors.)

2. Have a punctuation contest. Set a time limit for this activity. See which group can form a sentence containing the most examples of internal punctuation and commas (only one example per rule).

3. Look in a book by Dickens or Sir Walter Scott or in the Bible, King James Version, and notice the punctuation used. Find any examples of the way we punctuate today and compare the two.

Section 3: Modifiers

1. Discussion questions:

   a. If English didn't have modifiers, it would be a very dull language.
      What kinds of sentences can you write which don't have modifiers? (One- and two-word sentences such as, "Come.", and "Birds fly.")

   b. Why are adjectives and adverbs called *modifiers*? (Modifiers change the meaning of a word by making it more definite.)

2. Start with five simple sentences. (Example: Babies cry.) Each member of the group is to add modifiers to the sentence. You might have "prizes" for the most interesting, most poetic, most ridiculous, most scholarly, and so forth.

Section 4: Coordination and Subordination

1. Discussion questions:

   a. Both coordination and subordination are used to make comparisons.
      What do each compare? (Coordination compares words and ideas of equal value. Subordination compares language elements which are not equal.)

   b. What happens to a sentence when a relative clause does not closely follow the word it modifies? Example: There is a flower in the vase which smells very nice. (The relative clause appears to modify the wrong word and the sentence is illogical. The flower, not the vase, smells very nice.)

2. Play a coordination game. Write out a set of twenty coordinating terms: *night* and *day*, *up* and *down*, and so forth. Call out the first word to the other group. If the other group supplies the correct answer it is their turn. The team answering the most wins.

3. Make a poster or cartoon demonstrating the idea of subordination.

Administer the LIFEPAC Spelling Test.
The test is provided in this Teacher's Guide.
Evaluate the tests and review the words the students spelled incorrectly.
If necessary, review all of the words in the unit to prepare for the alternate spelling test.
Administer the Alternate LIFEPAC Spelling test that is provided in this Teacher's Guide.

Administer the LIFEPAC Test.
The test is to be administered in one session. Give no help except with directions.
Evaluate the tests and review areas where the students have done poorly.
Review the pages and activities that stress the concepts tested.
If necessary, administer the Alternate LIFEPAC Test.

ANSWER KEYS

SECTION 1

1.1 Whenever, I, "The Night Before Christmas," This, December, John, Cindy, I, Arizona, They, North, Lincoln Road, Phoenix, Arizona, On, Christmas Eve, First Christian Church, Later, Mr., Mrs. Simpson

1.2 John said to ted, "please give me the wrench."

1.3 last summer we went to colorado and visited Denver, Vail, and two other Cities.

1.4 The scene I'd like to see
is an elephant in a tree,
He'd be looking for his kite
wouldn't that be a sight?

1.5 Mary and She drank pepsi as they watched the Football game.

1.6 do you like french fried potatoes?

1.7 Have you ever seen the Pacific ocean?

1.8 My Family is from farmington, west Virginia.

1.9 Washington school is located on Main street.

1.10 Many of the members of our Church Youth Group are also members of the Philadelphia youth band.

1.11 My family attends Trinity Lutheran church.

1.12 The second friday in june is the last Day of school.

1.13 World war II was fought in the twentieth century.

1.14 The U.S. constitution is a blueprint of our Government.

1.15 I asked mother if my Father was home yet.

1.16 "The gift of the Magi" is my favorite short story.

1.17 Doreen and i frequently went swimming last Summer.

1.18 The holy trinity consists of God the father, the Son, and the Holy spirit.

1.19 Do You understand spanish?

1.20 My older brother is taking algebra 2, english, Wood Shop, History, Physical Education, and religion at his high school.

1.21 Christmas is both a Holiday and a holy day.

1.22-1.36 Examples:

1.22 Frank replied, "The skiing lesson begins at 7:30 in the morning."

1.23 Have you heard of the wonderful one-hoss shay,
That was built in such a logical way,
It ran a hundred years to a day,
And then, of a sudden - it - oh, but stay.

1.24 Mark, Steve, and Fred played the guard positions.

1.25 I brought a package each of Wise, Planters, and Lay's potato chips.

1.26 Some early Christians were persecuted by the Romans.

1.27 Mr. Philip Stevenson
605 Columbus Avenue
Seattle, Washington, U.S.A.

1.28 Atlantic Ocean
Roosevelt Lake
Blue Ridge
Missouri River

1.29 George Washington High School

1.30 On Wednesday, December 25, we will celebrate the birth of Christ, which we call Christmas.

1.31 The Declaration of Independence
The Fourth of July
The Settlement of Jamestown

1.32 Rev. H.L. Davis
Dr. J.A. Moreland
Mrs. Vivian Jones

1.33 Mother and Father are visiting my sister

1.34 "Somewhere Over the Rainbow"

1.35 In my Father's house are many mansions.

1.36 French, Spanish, Russian

1.37 Vacationing, Virginia, I, Blue Ridge Mountains, Dad, Peaks, Otter

Wait, I, Lake, Monroe

Last, Timothy

Soon, Evanston, Illinois, Dr. Miller, Charlottesville, University, Virginia, The, Millers, Virginia, June, July, August, Their, Mary, Linda

Together, Shenandoah Valley, We, Natural Bridge, President Woodrow Wilson's, Staunton, Washington, Lee, Lexington, What, General Robert E. Lee's, Traveler

1.38 In the beginning God created the heavens and the earth.

1.39 <u>Adjectives</u>
quick
careful
extreme
angry
final
slow
happy
quiet

<u>Adverbs</u>
quickly
carefully
extremely
finally
slowly
happily
quietly
somewhat
already

<u>Adjective or Adverb</u>
happier
quieter
backward
friendly
early
daily
fast

1.40 Either order:
a. er
b. ly

1.41-1.43 Examples:
1.41 a. The quick fox escaped.
b. The final decision has been reached.
c. The slow turtle was quite large.
1.42 a. Jimmy whistled happily.
b. Cindy has finally finished the lesson.
c. Lori was extremely careful with her painting.
1.43 a. Peggy is much happier now.
b. The friendly puppy ran to me.
c. We read the Bible daily.

SELF TEST 1

1.01 true
1.02 false
1.03 false
1.04 false
1.05 true
1.06 a
1.07 a
1.08 a
1.09 b
1.10 b
1.011 a
1.012 b
1.013 a
1.014 a
1.015 a
1.016 a
1.017 b
1.018 Bill said "<u>today</u> is <u>friday</u>."
1.019 Our (Family) enjoys <u>german</u> food.
1.020 The Midville <u>library</u> is located near the (Park) on Elm <u>avenue</u>.
1.021 This (Winter) Father is going to buy us a sled.
1.022 Next year <u>i'm</u> going to study <u>latin</u>.

SECTION 2

2.1 Jim's bicycle is missing and <u>his</u> paper route's collections have also disappeared.

2.2 The voter's duty is to appear at <u>his</u> district's polls on Tuesday.

2.3 Freshmen's textbooks are always the last to be distributed.

2.4 Mother's cakes never remain in <u>her</u> kitchen very long.

2.5 You get <u>your</u> dollar's worth at the discount store's sale.

2.6 somebody<u>'s</u> pencil

2.7 Bob<u>'s</u> skates

2.8 the two boy<u>s'</u> ball

2.9 sheep<u>'s</u> wool

2.10 a week<u>'s</u> vacation

2.11 Bob<u>'s</u> and Mary<u>'s</u> houses

2.12 Smith and West<u>'s</u> Pharmacy

2.13 women<u>'s</u> cakes

2.14 a dollar<u>'s</u> worth of candy

2.15 Sandy and Regina<u>'s</u> radio

2.16 no one<u>'s</u> fault

2.17 the three chair<u>s'</u> legs

2.18 Fred, Frank, and Harry<u>'s</u> basketball

2.19 mother<u>'s</u> car

2.20 can't

2.21 don't

2.22 he'll

2.23 I'll

2.24 it's

2.25 she'd

2.26 shouldn't

2.27 they're

2.28 we're

2.29 won't

2.30-2.37 Examples:

2.30 Someone's coat was found in the lobby.

2.31 The rug's design is oriental.

2.32 Our children's friends are welcome here.

2.33 Most cars' license plates are out of state.

2.34 Bill and Jack's boat needs a good paint job.

2.35 Tom's and Ted's pencils are missing.

2.36 It's raining outside, isn't it?

2.37 The r's and s's have more names listed below them.

2.38 I've, today's, It's, mother's, paper's, ladies', father's, editors', (or editor's), He's, readers', I'm, doesn't, can't anyone's, someone's, day's

2.39 Brent said, "It is getting late."

2.40 "Today is Friday," said Mary Lou, "and we have a three day vacation from school."

2.41 "Have you ever seen an alligator?" asked Wendy.

2.42 "I can't go with you," said Fred. "Thank you for asking me."

2.43 "When I was your age," my father said, "I had to walk seven miles in the snow to get to school, and it was uphill both ways!"

2.44 He read a poem entitled "The Prayer of the Little Bird."

2.45 Are you familiar with Hans Christian Andersen's "The Emperor's New Clothes?"

2.46 His favorite hymn is "Onward, Christian Soldiers."

2.47 Did you read the article "Human Rights on Trial" in *Time* Magazine?

2.48 I listened to "The Six O'Clock News" on station KFLR.

2.49 She is as "sweet" as lemon juice.

2.50 That is really "hot."

2.51-2.60 Examples:

2.51 These are her words, "Take a side and defend your statements."

2.52 She said that we should take a side and defend it.

2.53 "Drive to Fifth Street," directed the policemen, "and go north to Elm Street."

2.54 "How much does it cost to mail the package first class?" I asked. "Let's see," said the postman, "that will be $1.97."

2.55 "Invictus"

2.56 "The Tell Tale Heart"

2.57 "The Mechanics of English: Part II"

2.58 "Carolina Moon"

2.59 "Guerrilla Tactics in El Salvador"

2.60 His budget felt the "pinch" at the end of the month.

2.61 Teacher check

2.62 Example:
He that believes in the Son has everlasting life.

2.63 twenty-eight, forty-seven, sixty-five

2.64 Example:
The recipe calls for one-third cup of water.

2.65 Example:
His behavior is anti-Christian.

2.66 Example:
Mary is an ex-teacher from Lincoln High.

2.67 Example:
My brother-in-law is a lawyer.

2.68 Mary, please wash the dishes.

2.69 Yes, I like to play tennis.

2.70 Before she cooked the breakfast, Mother read her Bible.

2.71 Near the end of the first week, we had earned enough money for our camping trip.

2.72 Sliding into third base, David tries to avoid the tag.

2.73 no comma required

2.74 Quietly, Sandy tiptoed out of the room.

2.75 Sad and discouraged, Julia wanted to be alone.

2.76 Dogs are nice, but you must take good care of them.

2.77 Bill must study for his test, or he will not get a good grade.

2.78 no comma required

2.79 no comma required

2.80 no comma required

2.81 false

2.82 true

2.83 false

2.84 true

2.85 true

2.86 false

2.87 true

2.88 Cold and wet, we rushed to warm ourselves around the fire.

2.89 No, we will not be able to go.

2.90 After I finish my homework, I will watch the high school football game.

2.91 Mark likes to play tennis, and I like to play soccer.

2.92 Bob likes to play football, of course.

2.93 John, the captain of our football team, dislocated his shoulder.

2.94 When we board the bus, Frank looks for a seat by a window.

2.95 Richard, on the other hand, does not enjoy ice skating.

2.96 By and large, most teen-age boys are big eaters.

2.97 Dr. Williams, a dentist, is very skillful.

2.98 no comma required

2.99 Mrs. Sullivan, who is my piano teacher, has thirty students.

2.100 no comma required

2.101 We ate ice cream, cake, and candy.

2.102 Josephine, Alice, or Juliane will correct the tests.

2.103 no comma required

2.104 I brushed my teeth, cleaned my nails, and combed my hair.

2.105 no comma required

2.106 We went to the store and bought meat, vegetables, fruit, bread, canned goods, milk, eggs, and sugar.

2.107 My favorite ice creams are strawberry, chocolate, butter pecan, and peppermint.

2.108 Ted, answer the phone please.

2.109 Dr. Warren, our family dentist, lives across the street.

2.110 On May 6, 2015, I moved to St. Louis, Missouri.

2.111 That information, in my opinion, is totally incorrect.

2.112 Yes, I bought fruit, cookies, lettuce, and bread in the grocery store.

2.113 Uncle Jack, the man in the blue suit, is a college professor.
or
Uncle Jack, the man in the blue suit is a college professor.

2.114 We ran the first three miles, but we walked the last two miles to the beach.

2.115 Tommy, my little brother, can read, write, add, subtract, and multiply.
or
Tommy, my little brother can read, write, add, subtract, and multiply.

2.116 On the way home we found the road to be rocky, narrow, and dangerous.

2.117-2.131 Examples:

2.117 Fred, where have you gone?

2.118 Where, Fred, have you gone?
Where have you gone, Fred?

2.119 Yes, we will attend the meeting.

2.120 Well, it's about time you came!

2.121 Running in the relay, Bob tripped and fell.

2.122 Dry and warm, the puppy slept all night.

2.123 Angrily, the mob demanded a refund.

2.124 The water is cold, but the sand is warm.

2.125 Jean painted with watercolors and listened to music.

2.126 We, on the other hand, enjoy reading good books.

2.127 The sky is blue, generally speaking.

2.128 Mr. Miller, the dean of the school, makes you feel very humble.

2.129 The car that he is driving has just been polished.

2.130 The clown in the center, who fell from the trapeze, seems rather dazed.

2.131 Carol, wanting to become better acquainted, invited the girls home.

2.132 a. _A_
b. _QM_
c. _C_
d. _H_
e. _P_
f. _C_

2.133 Teacher check

2.134 Sentences will vary.
Examples:
a. That is a *man's* sweater.
b. Set off *parenthetic* expressions with commas.
c. *They're* all finished with their work.
d. California borders the *Pacific Ocean*.
e. *I'm* ready to go.
f. I made *seventy-four* dollars last summer.
g. Did you see them play in the *all-star* game?
h. *February* is the shortest month.
i. *No one* was in the room.
j. The *Chinese* ping-pong team is very quick.
k. He testified before the committee of *un-American* activities.
l. The week is half gone by *Wednesday*.
m. Dad's *mother-in-law* is my grandmother.
n. They thought he *couldn't* finish the race.

2.135 Across
1. Christian
2. nonrestrictive
6. December
8. I'm
9. ladies'
10. man's
11. theirs

Down
1. Canadian
3. Tuesday
4. children's
5. everyone
7. Chinese

SELF TEST 2

2.01 false
2.02 true
2.03 false
2.04 false
2.05 true
2.06 _QM_
2.07 _C_
2.08 _A_
2.09 _H_
2.010 _C_
2.011 _P_
2.012 _QM_
2.013 _A_
2.014 _H_
2.015 _P_
2.016 The martins just returned from sweden.
2.017 The Government is attempting to make Reforms.
2.018 In the Summer we will vacation at lake powell.
2.019 This Semester I'm taking math, History latin, and english.
2.020 The library of congress is located in washington.
2.021 Mother said, "Mary, please come here."
2.022 My mother's new outfit (it's blue) is pretty.
2.023 This evening's dinner will consist of soup, salad, a main course, and a dessert.
2.024 Before Carl answered the telephone, he closed the door.
2.025 Slowly and deliberately, Sandy stated that she hopes (as we all do) that Nancy will come to know Jesus.
2.026 You can come with us, or you can stay at your uncle's house.
2.027 Generally speaking, the ladies' Bible study lasts forty-five minutes.
2.028 "If you want to go with us," said Jack, "you must be at my house on time."
2.029 Our pastor, a man of much learning, attended Yale Divinity School.
2.030 Yes, we all sang "The Star Spangled Banner."
2.031-2.035 Sentences will vary.
Examples:
2.031 The *clarity* of their voices was amazing.
2.032 Write out the *dialogue* of the characters.
2.033 The historical *document* was missing.
2.034 Adding ginger to the recipe is *optional*.
2.035 The *plural* of tooth is teeth.

SECTION 3

3.1	The lamp is on the table.
3.2	On the table is the lamp.
3.3	I read a good book.
3.4	Bill and Mark played ping-pong.
3.5	Coming down the street was Mr. Jones.
3.6	This old radio words very well.
3.7	I am tired.
3.8	Walking on the roof were two birds.
3.9	There is my new bicycle.
3.10	Jack caught the ball.
3.11	She closed the door.
3.12	The chairs are new.
3.13	She will bake cookies.
3.14	We will be coming to your house.
3.15	The children are playing in the yard.
3.16	The old man
3.17	is eating a simple supper
3.18	man
3.19	is eating
3.20	supper
3.21	This month has been long.
3.22	My uncle drives a new car.
3.23	Bob, bring your books.
3.24	Steve can play the trumpet.
3.25	The children watched the animals.
3.26	true
3.27	false
3.28	false
3.29	false
3.30	true
3.31	true
3.32-3.35	Examples:
3.32	He is my good friend.
3.33	This is he (or she or I or we or they).
3.34	The tree is large.
3.35	Our team won the game.
3.36	Five cookies are on the table.
3.37	The small boy is afraid of dogs.
3.38	Kathy is helpful.
3.39	A second look will be helpful.
3.40	The boys, rude and loud, demanded milk.
3.41	Keith and Werner are big and strong.
3.42	The old man is tired.
3.43	An apple tastes good.
3.44	A few girls, only three, have ice skates.
3.45	That man is funny.

3.46-3.48	Examples:
3.46	The three kittens ran beneath the chair.
3.47	The old man boarded the bus.
3.48	These turkey eggs will hatch soon.
3.49	Teacher check
3.50	V I never use profanity.
3.51	V Mark sits there.
3.52	V Phil carefully drew a picture of a horse.
3.53	V Scott nearly fell from a tree.
3.54	ADV V Scott very nearly fell from a tree.
3.55	ADJ It's not nice to spit on the sidewalk.
3.56	ADV V ADJ She quite suddenly became very sad.
3.57-3.62	Examples:
3.57	He collects monthly for the paper.
3.58	There are the books.
3.59	The food disappeared rapidly.
3.60	They ate very quickly.
3.61	Mr. Jones is a very good teacher.
3.62	The food is not good.
3.63	true
3.64	false
3.65	true
3.66	false
3.67	Myron ran down the stairs.
3.68	He came over the hill and through the garden.
3.69	She will come to our house in the morning.
3.70	On the table is the book.
3.71	One of the girls brought some candy for you.
3.72-3.80	Examples:
3.72	The floor in the bedroom is dirty.
3.73	The basketball team from Phoenix plays well.
3.74	We need gloves for baseball.
3.75	They have tickets to (for) the circus.
3.76	John watched a game of basketball.
3.77	I will be there at twelve o'clock.
3.78	The game will be played in Boston.
3.79	Mary won the relay swimming under water.
3.80	She lay in the sun for several hours.
3.81	Teacher check

SELF TEST 3

3.01   a
3.02   a
3.03   a
3.04   b
3.05   b
3.06   d
3.07   f
3.08   b
3.09   a
3.010   d
3.011   Yes, we all sang "The Star Spangled Banner."
3.012   You can go with us, or you can stay with your cousin.
3.013   Before Joy answered the telephone, she closed the door.
3.014   Tonight's dinner will include soup, salad, main course, and dessert.
3.015   Father said, "Jon, please come here."
3.016   true
3.017   false
3.018   false
3.019   true
3.020   true
3.021   false
3.022   false
3.023   true
3.024   true
3.025   true
3.026   a
3.027   b
3.028   b
3.029   c
3.030   b
3.031   subject
3.032   object
3.033   prepositional
3.034   subject
3.035   nominative
3.036-3.038 Examples:
3.036   The brown Bible belongs to Jeffrey.
3.037   My Bible is blue.
3.038   Did you read your Bible today?

SECTION 4

4.1-4.10 Examples:
4.1   eggs
4.2   she
4.3   England
4.4   cry
4.5   conversed or chatted
4.6   were
4.7   unhappy
4.8   third
4.9   loudly
4.10   down
4.11-4.17 Examples:
4.11   <u>Mom and Dad</u> went to church.
4.12   The boys <u>skipped and hopped</u> all the way home.
4.13   She <u>washed the dishes</u> and <u>polished the silver</u>.
4.14   Jesus is our <u>Saviour</u> and <u>Lord</u>.
4.15   <u>Joe and Bill</u> <u>swam and sailed</u> all day.
4.16   <u>Beth and Linda</u> <u>have been shopping</u> and <u>will go swimming</u>.
4.17   <u>He and I</u> saw <u>monkeys and elephants</u>.
4.18-4.20 Examples:
4.18   The <u>brown and white</u> dress is <u>lovely</u>.
4.19   We ate the <u>ripe and mellow</u> cantaloupe.
4.20   <u>Quickly and quietly</u> they filed inside.
4.21   Teacher check
4.22-4.27 Examples:
4.22   at home.
4.23   the pen with the red ink are mine.
4.24   stared at the clock.
4.25   feeding the pigeons
4.26   to play
4.27   Teacher check
4.28-4.29 Examples:
4.28   because the wind is blowing.
4.29   if someone will do my chores.
4.30   Example:
     Because it is <u>cold and rainy</u> and because we don't want to be sick, we will not go. (cause relationship)
4.31   a.   and
     b.   or (and)
     c.   Example:
        Tom will ride his bicycle, or he will walk to school.
4.32   a.   The birds fly south for the winter; they return in the spring.
     b.   I like dogs; I also like cats.
     c.   Example:
        The cattle went out into the pasture; they returned to the barn at night.

4.33 Examples:
    a. ; therefore, (consequently)
    b. ; in fact, (indeed,) and so forth
    c. Example:
        New cars have many defects; in fact, old ones may give less trouble.

4.34-4.38 Examples:
4.34 unless you go with me
4.35 Because we needed groceries for dinner
4.36 who had just won the tennis match
4.37 who is wearing the blue, tweed suit
4.38 "How to Lose Weight By Dieting"

4.39-4.43 Examples:
4.39 After we attend the concert, we are going out to eat.
4.40 Tom is returning from Europe after he spends New Year's Eve in Paris.
4.41 When it stops raining, we will go to the park, if you want to go.
4.42 When you find the street that crosses Wilshire, you are nearly there.
4.43 I have the map in my car, which is the grey sedan that is in the garage.

4.44-4.46 Examples:
4.44 When Jesus died on the Cross, He bore our sins; and He made possible our salvation.
4.45 The visitors arrived at the airport, and they went directly to a hotel that is near the ocean.
4.46 They will attend church where their son is a pastor, and they will probably move their membership there.
4.47 Teacher check
4.48 <u>Dogs</u> <u>that bark</u> annoy me.
4.49 I like <u>candy</u> <u>that is sour</u>.
4.50 <u>People</u> <u>whose minds are on the Lord</u> usually lead good lives.
4.51 John is a <u>person</u> <u>whom we like</u>.

4.52-4.56 Examples:
4.52 I enjoy books that are biographies.
4.53 People who are rude lose friends quickly.
4.54 He goes to Italian restaurants which feature ravioli.
4.55 The bus driver whose wallet was lost is quite upset.
4.56 I like people whom I can trust.
4.57 Teacher check

4.58 Examples:

Word	Synonym
a. abundance	plenty
b. acquaintance	friend
c. bargain	barter
d. beautiful	attractive
e. conquer	overcome (defeat)
f. definitely	absolutely
g. handkerchief	bandana
h. gasoline	fuel
i. loneliness	solitude
j. marriage	wedding
k. municipal	city
l. pleasant	enjoyable
m. restaurant	cafe
n. rhythm	beat
o. column	post

4.59 Teacher check

SELF TEST 4

4.01   true
4.02   false
4.03   true
4.04   true
4.05   false
4.06   _Adv_
4.07   _Adj_
4.08   _N_
4.09   _V_
4.010 _P_
4.011 _Adj_
4.012 _Adv_
4.013 _P_
4.014 _N_
4.015 _V_
4.016 d
4.017 g
4.018 f
4.019 i
4.020 e
4.021 h
4.022 b
4.023 a
4.024 _C_
4.025 _S_
4.026 _S_
4.027 _C_
4.028 jack said, "mother, may i have seventy-five cents?"
4.029 last wednesday, john and i saw "the today show."
4.030 the children's siamese cat (it's brown) is an all-star pest.
4.031 the ladies' meeting will be held at the first christian church on august 3.
4.032 steve told us he is studying spanish at cleveland christian school, which is located on third street.
4.033 "if you want to be successful," said father, "do your best, but you should never worry that your best isn't good enough."
4.034-4.038 Examples:
4.034 Mr. Fields is an amateur golfer.
4.035 Mary is an efficient secretary.
4.036 Include your middle initial.
4.037 Adverbs may modify adjectives, verbs, and other adverbs.
4.038 These ideas are not related.

LIFEPAC TEST

1. true
2. false
3. false
4. true
5. false
6. true
7. false
8. false
9. true
10. true
11. _QM_
12. _P_
13. _A_
14. _C_
15. _H_
16. c, d
17. c, d
18. a, d
19. b, c
20. a, c, d
21. The old man jumped up and down.
22. Mother put beans in the jar.
23. I am happy.
24. She is very happy.
25. To spit on the sidewalk is not nice.
26. compound
27. complex
28. complex
29. compound
30. compound
31. place
32. time
33. requirement
34. cause

ALTERNATE LIFEPAC TEST

1. c
2. g
3. k
4. i
5. b
6. h
7. j
8. e
9. f
10. a
11. Christian faith imparts moral courage to believers.
12. The United States Constitution is a blueprint for government.
13. The second Friday in June is the day of our class picnic.
14. The small puppy chased the ball across the floor.
15. One day our favorite cousin came home unexpectedly.
16. compound sentence
17. subordinating conjunctions
18. relative clause
19. true
20. false
21. true
22. true
23. false
24. b
25. c
26. b
27. d
28. c
29. a
30. d
31. a
32. Example:
   Modify means to change or limit the meaning of a word.
33. Example:
   A *hyphen* is a mark of punctuation used between compound words, syllables, certain prefixes and nouns, compound numbers, and certain fractions.

SPELLING TEST

1	quick	How **quick** is your delivery service?	quick
2	careful	Be **careful** when you lift that box.	careful
3	carefully	She **carefully** prepared the dinner.	carefully
4	extremely	The dog is **extremely** mean.	extremely
5	final	The **final** test is harder than the first one.	final
6	finally	We **finally** made it to the picnic grounds.	finally
7	slowly	The runners ran **slowly** up the mountainside.	slowly
8	happier	His family seems to be **happier** than ours.	happier
9	quiet	The librarian told us to be **quiet**.	quiet
10	quieter	Our room was **quieter** than the next one.	quieter
11	backward	He rode his bike **backward**.	backward
12	early	We had to get up **early** for the camping trip.	early
13	somewhat	She is **somewhat** of an expert on the topic.	somewhat
14	fast	How **fast** can he go on his bike?	fast
15	yours	Is this book **yours** or mine?	yours
16	Canadian	She is not French but **Canadian**.	Canadian
17	parenthetic	She told us not to use a **parenthetic** clause.	parenthetic
18	no one	**No one** has seen Jim for several days.	no one
19	seventy-four	My grandfather is **seventy-four** years old.	seventy-four
20	theirs	That book is **theirs**.	theirs
21	all-star	The **all-star** team prepared for the game.	all-star
22	February	In **February** I will be celebrating my birthday.	February
23	nonessential	That word is **nonessential** to the story.	nonessential
24	Chinese	Is she **Chinese**?	Chinese
25	nonrestrictive	That is a **nonrestrictive** clause.	nonrestrictive
26	un-American	They said that he was **un-American**.	un-American
27	mother-in-law	My **mother-in-law** is coming to visit.	mother-in-law
28	children's	The **children's** stories are delightful.	children's

SPELLING TEST

29	couldn't	He **couldn't** stay for dinner.	couldn't
30	abundance	There is an **abundance** of wealth in the United States.	abundance
31	acquaintance	She is an **acquaintance** of mine.	acquaintance
32	amateur	That team is not a professional one but an **amateur** one.	amateur
33	beautiful	What a **beautiful** sunset!	beautiful
34	business	What **business** is he in?	business
35	column	He writes a **column** for the local newspaper.	column
36	definitely	They **definitely** wanted to see the game.	definitely
37	efficient	Tom is an **efficient** worker.	efficient
38	gasoline	**Gasoline** prices are increasing.	gasoline
39	handkerchief	May I use your **handkerchief**?	handkerchief
40	license	He just received his driver's **license**.	license
41	loneliness	Jesus said he could cure man's problem of **loneliness**.	loneliness
42	marriage	Sue plans to have her **marriage** in the summer.	marriage
43	orchestra	The **orchestra** played one of Beethoven's pieces.	orchestra
44	restaurant	We ate at an Italian **restaurant**.	restaurant
45	rhythm	That poem has good **rhythm**.	rhythm

LANGUAGE ARTS 706

ALTERNATE LIFEPAC TEST

NAME _____

DATE _____

SCORE _____

58

73

Match these items (each answer, 2 points).

1. _____ apostrophe

2. _____ comma

3. _____ hyphen

4. _____ parenthesis

5. _____ quotation marks

6. _____ relative pronouns

7. _____ subordination

8. _____ conjunctive adverbs

9. _____ adverb

10. _____ absolute phrase

a. a group of words having no grammatical relationship to any other word in a sentence

b. used with titles of songs and poems

c. shows possession or contraction

d. words that tell who or what receives the action of the verb

e. used with a semicolon to join two independent clauses

f. modifies the simple predicate

g. used after introductory words

h. introduces an adjective clause

i. enclose supplementary or explanatory information

j. makes an idea less important by letting it depend on another independent idea

k. is used between some compound words

Underline the simple subject once, the simple predicate twice, and circle the complement (each sentence, 3 points).

11.   Christian faith imparts moral courage to believers.

12.   The United States Constitution is a blueprint of our government.

13.   The second Friday in June is the day of our class picnic.

Underline adjectives once, adverbs twice, and circle prepositional phrases (each sentence, 3 points).

14.   The small puppy chased the ball across the floor.

15.   One day our favorite cousin came home unexpectedly.

Complete these sentences (each answer, 3 points).

16.   A sentence with two independent clauses is a(n) _____ .

17.   Words such as *when, after, where, because,* and *since* are called _____
       _____ .

18.   An adjective clause introduced by such words as *who, whom,* or *which* is called a(n)
       _____ .

Answer *true* or *false* (each answer, 1 point).

19.   _____ Always capitalize the first word of a direct quotation.

20.   _____ Capitalize the names of subjects.

21.   _____ The words *mother* and *father* should not always be capitalized.

22.   _____ The names of specific historical periods, events, dates, and documents
       should be capitalized.

23.   _____ Capitalize all the words in titles.

Write the letter for the correct answer on each line (each answer, 2 points).

24. Which sentence is correctly punctuated? _____
    a. After Sue washed her hair; she borrowed Joan's hair dryer.
    b. Before today he had never eaten snails.
    c. Could'nt you come to see us Friday?
    d. His 8s are hard to read.

25. Which sentence is correctly punctuated? _____
    a. Have you read the poem "The Pasture"?
    b. A three fourths majority, however, is needed for the bill to pass.
    c. Gary Miller led an anti-Russian movement.
    d. Yes I'll go with you.

26. Which sentence contains a relative clause? _____
    a. Happy and warm, the baby quickly fell asleep.
    b. The boy who borrowed my coat is my friend.
    c. Since we are ready, we ought to go.
    d. If you want to be successful, do your best.

27. Which sentence contains *incorrect* coordination? _____
    a. Bill and Sally plan to go to Texas or Alaska.
    b. The puppy was cute and fluffy.
    c. I will arrive in the morning or in the afternoon.
    d. I will be finished but quick!

28. The word *nonrestrictive* means _____ .
    a. without rules   b. emphatic
    c. not necessary   d. confirmed

29. The word *parenthetic* means _____ .
    a. ideas not closely related to the rest of the sentence
    b. information necessary to sentence meaning
    c. a pause
    d. optional

30. The correctly spelled word is _____ .
    a. abundence   b. calander
    c. conquor   d. amateur

31. The correctly spelled word is _____ .
    a. orchestra   b. municaple
    c. desparate   d. restaraunt

Write a clear, complete sentence defining each of the these terms (each answer, 4 points).

32.   modify _____

_____

33.   hyphen _____

_____

ALTERNATE SPELLING TEST

1	quickly	He **quickly** ran up the hill.	quickly
2	extreme	She had an **extreme** case of the flu.	extreme
3	angry	Why is his father **angry**?	angry
4	slow	**Slow** down when you come to a stop sign.	slow
5	happy	The baby is very **happy**.	happy
6	happily	He **happily** went on his way.	happily
7	quietly	My sister **quietly** slipped out the room.	quietly
8	friendly	That dog is very **friendly**.	friendly
9	daily	He runs two miles **daily**.	daily
10	already	He has **already** left for home.	already
11	Tuesday	On **Tuesday** we will be going to California.	Tuesday
12	everyone	**Everyone** had a good time at the park.	everyone
13	man's	**Man's** best friend is said to be the dog.	man's
14	they're	**They're** planning on leaving next week.	they're
15	Pacific Ocean	The **Pacific Ocean** lies off the California coast.	Pacific Ocean
16	I'm	**I'm** going to be in high school next year.	I'm
17	seventy-four	My grandfather is **seventy-four** years old.	seventy-four
18	Christian	She is a **Christian**.	Christian
19	February	In **February** I will be celebrating my birthday.	February
20	nonessential	That word is **nonessential** to the story.	nonessential
21	ladies'	The **ladies'** cakes were very good.	ladies'
22	nonrestrictive	That is a **nonrestrictive** clause.	nonrestrictive
23	Wednesday	**Wednesday** was the day set for the baseball game.	Wednesday
24	December	**December** went by fast.	December
25	couldn't	He **couldn't** stay for dinner.	couldn't
26	abundance	There is an **abundance** of wealth in the United States.	abundance
27	acquaintance	She is an **acquaintance** of mine.	acquaintance
28	bargain	That bake sale was a **bargain**.	bargain

ALTERNATE SPELLING TEST

29	beautiful	What a **beautiful** sunset.	beautiful
30	business	What **business** is he in?	business
31	calendar	We received our new **calendar** yesterday.	calendar
32	conquer	She had to **conquer** her fears.	conquer
33	desperate	He was a **desperate** criminal.	desperate
34	efficient	Tom is an **efficient** worker.	efficient
35	foreign	Rick works on **foreign** cars.	foreign
36	definitely	They **definitely** wanted to see the game.	definitely
37	government	The **government** is trying to decrease prices.	government
38	initial	He made his **initial** move to the basket.	initial
39	handkerchief	May I use your **handkerchief**?	handkerchief
40	license	He just received his driver's **license**.	license
41	loneliness	Jesus said he could cure man's problem of **loneliness**.	loneliness
42	municipal	They went to the **municipal** courthouse.	municipal
43	orchestra	The **orchestra** played one of Beethoven's pieces.	orchestra
44	restaurant	We ate at an Italian **restaurant**.	restaurant
45	pleasant	The flowers had a **pleasant** aroma.	pleasant

LANGUAGE ARTS 707

Unit 7: The Hiding Place: A Study Guide

TEACHER NOTES

MATERIALS NEEDED FOR LIFEPAC	
Required	Suggested
None	• encyclopedia • history books • maps • dictionary • Corrie ten Boom, with John and Elizabeth Sherrill. *The Hiding Place*. Lincoln, VA: Chosen Books, Ltd., 1971 (or any other edition available). • reference books or online sources

ADDITIONAL LEARNING ACTIVITIES

Section 1: Normal Life

1. Obtain a map of Western Europe (a wall-hung map is best) and point out various countries—Holland, France, Germany. (social studies)

2. Arrange for a person who is familiar with Holland or with war-time Europe to visit the students and present some information about the war, the countries, and the people. (social studies)

3. Find out about Holland's natural resources and if they were of any use of Germany in their war effort. (social studies)

4. Discuss this question: Why was it strategic for Germany to occupy Holland? (social studies)

5. Write a letter to the Dutch embassy, United Nations, or the common market asking questions about topics you are interested in. (social studies)

6. Create a display of the Dutch, German, and other European flags. Discuss the history of these flags.

7. Using an historical atlas and a blank map, locate and identify the boundaries of European countries during World War II.

8. Create your own map of Europe as if Hitler had won the war.

9. Using an atlas, geography book, online resources, and a blank map, locate and identify the countries of Europe as they exist today.

10. Design a bookmark to accompany the ideas in *The Hiding Place*. Illustrate this with characters from the book or any design you wish.

11. Obtain an interview of anyone who lived during World War II in an occupied country. Write a news story or feature story based on your interview.

Section 2: Secret Hiding

1. Find a copy of one of Dickens' books and read some of his descriptions of characters to the students. Discuss personality traits.

2. Discussion questions:

    a. What if Hitler had been assassinated before the end of the war?

    b. What if America had been conquered by Hitler?

    c. What if Corrie and her family had not been willing to help the Jews?

    d. What if no one had been willing to help the Jews?

    e. What if Hitler had hated Christians instead of Jews?

3. Create a mural about life in Holland during the war or about a related topic.

4. Dramatize a German interrogation using Corrie's experiences as a basis.

5. Draw the plans of the Beje or make a cardboard model, showing the watch shop, living quarters, and the hiding place.

6. Make a time line of Hitler's conquest of Europe.

7. Write a news story about a war event as the Germans would have reported that event. Then rewrite the story reporting the event as the Dutch would have done it.

8. Make a recording as though you were reporting news of the war in a radio broadcast.

9. Draw a political cartoon based on the war. For example, you could draw one about the interaction of the Dutch and the German soldiers.

10. Examine pictures of costumes and clothing worn during World War II.
    Prepare a costume to show the students or draw a sketch of such a costume.

11. Compose a short jingle or song portraying Dutch patriotism.

Section 3: Cruel Imprisonment

1. Present to the students any information you have about early prisons. For instance, prisons in Bible times were usually underground, often caves or pits. These prisons were windowless and small. The prisoners were generally chained.

2. Discuss the persecution of the Jews at various times in history.

3. How do you think Corrie would have responded if she was asked if the Germans were her friends when she was in the concentration camp? How would you have responded?

4. If you had been Corrie, would you have planned an escape from the concentration camp?

5. Find Bible references to imprisonment and persecution. What does the Bible tell Christians about these trials? Write a paper on this subject.

Administer the LIFEPAC Spelling Test.

The test is provided in this Teacher's Guide.

Evaluate the tests and review the words the students spelled incorrectly.

If necessary, review all of the words in the unit to prepare for the alternate spelling test.

Administer the Alternate LIFEPAC Spelling test that is provided in this Teacher's Guide.

Administer the LIFEPAC Test.

The test is to be administered in one session. Give no help except with directions.

Evaluate the tests and review areas where the students have done poorly.

Review the pages and activities that stress the concepts tested.

If necessary, administer the Alternate LIFEPAC Test.

ANSWER KEYS

SECTION 1

1.1   c

1.2   a

1.3   i

1.4   f

1.5   e

1.6   g

1.7   d

1.8   h

1.9   Example:
"And so the shadow fell across us..."
the fourth paragraph from the end (p15)

1.10   true

1.11   true

1.12   false

1.13   true

1.14   false

1.15   She realized that death is real when she felt the cold hand. She began to fear the death of loved ones, especially her father.

1.16   He said that God would give her the strength she needed just in time—just as he gave her her train ticket just before they got on the train to Amsterdam.

1.17   a.   4
       b.   2
       c.   5
       d.   3
       e.   1
       f.   6

1.18   love

1.19   a.   kill the love and let a part of himself die
       b.   ask God to provide another way for love to go

1.20   Twenty Questions

1.21   a.   Karel
       b.   his wife

1.22   began singing "Fairest Lord Jesus," her favorite hymn

1.23   died in her sleep

1.24   licensed woman watchmaker

1.25   yes, no, and Corrie

1.26   Nollie's wedding

1.27   Corrie's father cared very much for everyone—but especially for his children. He was willing to spend time with them and since he constantly read the Bible and prayed and relied on God—God gave him wisdom.

1.28   For Corrie housekeeping was a chore, but for Betsie it was a joy—Betsie did wonderful things around the house.

1.29   Betsie did not enjoy keeping books, but Corrie loved the challenge of making the accounts balance and keeping track of work in the shop.

1.30   He persecuted him in many ways, such as talking down to him, calling him names, tripping him, hitting him, and ridiculing him.

1.31   Otto had forced Christoffels into the side of a building, pushing his face against its rough walls purposely.

1.32   false

1.33   false

1.34   true

1.35   true

1.36   false

1.37   Several airplanes were fighting over Haarlem. During the fight, Corrie went downstairs to join Betsie for tea. While she was gone a piece of shrapnel fell through the ceiling and onto her pillow.

1.38   Near the first part of the chapter Corrie says, "And it was then that I had the dream... Then as I watched... but we didn't want to go..."; and in the last two paragraphs of the fifth chapter she says, "And then an extraordinary thing happened. Even as I prayed...."

1.39   Teacher check

1.40   Teacher check

1.41   c

1.42   f

1.43   e

1.44   b

1.45   Any order:
       a.   physical features
       b.   conduct
       c.   outward appearance

1.46   a.   habits
       b.   personality
       c.   behavior

1.47   observation

1.48   Teacher check

1.49   *-ence, -ance,* and *-ness*

1.50   nouns

1.51   depend

1.52   rely

1.53   insure

1.54	accept
1.55	reside
1.56	hinder
1.57	effect
1.58	allow
1.59	comply
1.60	ally
1.61	resist

1.62-1.69 Examples:

1.62 The circumference of the earth is 24,901 miles.

1.63 His exuberance got him into trouble at school.

1.64 One should never give credence to gossip.

1.65 Intelligence is sometimes hard to measure.

1.66 The greatness of God cannot be measured.

1.67 It is good to use a concordance when you study the Bible.

1.68 Jerry was such a nuisance that he had very few friends.

1.69 The patience of Job is something we should all follow.

1.70	blessedness
1.71	brilliance
1.72	loveliness
1.73	musician
1.74	gratitude
1.75	patience
1.76	compliance
1.77	hindrance
1.78	resistance
1.79	allowance
1.80	acceptance
1.81	dependence

SELF TEST 1

1.01	d
1.02	e
1.03	c
1.04	i
1.05	a
1.06	j
1.07	b
1.08	g
1.09	f

1.010 a. Willem
b. Nollie
c. Betsie

1.011 hundredth anniversary of their watch shop

1.012 the Beje

1.013 radios

1.014 Any order:
a. physical features
b. conduct
c. outward appearance

1.015 a. actions
b. personality characteristics
c. behavior

1.016 do some very careful observation

1.017 a. _3_
b. _2_
c. _5_
d. _1_
e. _4_

1.018 Corrie took Betsie's place helping in the watch shop when Betsie was ill. As Betsie grew stronger, she assumed some of Corrie's former household chores. The sisters found they were much happier in their new roles.

1.019 Rumors of persecution were first revealed. Otto, the young German, persecuted Christoffels. Then active persecution by German soldiers came to the neighborhood.

1.020 Corrie's father taught his children about God's love and His purpose. They learned to give their problems to God and to extend Christian love to others.

SECTION 2

2.1	c	2.25	Eusie and the others as they stored their belongings in the hiding place
2.2	d	2.26	ill with influenza
2.3	c	2.27	prison bag filled with necessities
2.4	b	2.28	six hundred guilders (money)
2.5	a	2.29	Either order:

2.6 She had a friend who was in charge of issuing them. He arranged to have the food office "broken into" and he was even beaten to make the theft seem more realistic.

2.29 Either order:
a. help the prisoners
b. hide her briefcase

2.7 The Alpina sign on the windowsill gave the "all clear" signal.

2.30 to leave her prison bag
2.31 trap
2.32 thirty-five

2.8 It was a small space for hiding Jews and was in Corrie's bedroom. Another brick wall was added thirty inches in from the old one. The wall was painted to look aged and old bookshelves were put in front of the small opening.

2.33 leading the evening prayer
2.34 c
2.35 e
2.36 h
2.37 b
2.38 i
2.39 j

2.9 e
2.10 a
2.11 b
2.12 d
2.13 winter (cold)
2.14 Christoffels
2.15 the potato cellar

2.40 k
2.41 g
2.42 l
2.43 a
2.44 d
2.45 Examples; any order:

2.16 He was a Jew with a strongly Jewish face and walk. He was light-hearted, unselfish, and very sensitive to the needs of others.

2.45 Examples; any order:
a. kindness
b. loyalty
c. unselfishness
d. helpfulness
e. honesty

2.17 Example:
Loyalty and trustworthiness so that one would not have to worry about their telling something they should not tell. Unselfishness because everything would have to be shared. Good disposition, or good nature, because one would be difficult to live with who complained all the time.

2.46 Examples; any order:
a. grouchiness
b. laziness
c. dishonesty
d. selfishness
e. unkindness

2.18 There is no Psalm 166; therefore, he began with Psalm 100. Next he would have recited Psalm 66.

2.47 Example:
Pickwick had a very strange—even frightening—outward appearance; but he was generous, kind-hearted, and loving. All through the book he found thoughtful ways of helping Corrie when she especially needed it. He was realistic and believable. There are many people whose outward appearance is not a true indication of their inner personality.

2.19 was afraid to go near it
2.20 relaying messages to and from Nollie
2.21 were rescued
2.22 prayer

2.23 The group staying at the Beje burst into her room, flashed a flashlight in her eyes, and began questioning her. The main technique was surprise.

2.48 purpose
2.49 Either order:
a. carefully
b. slowly
2.50 essential details

2.24 He revealed his knowledge of her underground activities. Next he told her about an informer and asked if she knew anyone who would kill him. Her answer was to pray God would convince the man to remain loyal.

2.51 Any order:
  a. Concentrate on what the person is saying —don't let your mind wander.
  b. Ask, "What is the main point of what he is saying?"
  c. Ask, "What do I want to remember later?"
  d. Ask, "Do I agree with him? Why or why not?"
  e. Show interest so that the speaker is encouraged.

2.52 Any order:
  a. speak plainly
  b. comments should be relevant and/or to the point
  c. don't use too much time

2.53 Teacher check

2.54 *-ise, -ize,* and *-ate*

2.55 verbs

2.56 analysis

2.57 supervision

2.58 summary

2.59 minimization

2.60 exercise

2.61 extermination

2.62 creation

2.63 situation

2.64 meditation

2.65 legislature *or* legislation

2.66 justification

2.67
  a. an-a-lyze
  b. civ-i-lize
  c. cre-ate
  d. cre-mate
  e. dra-ma-tize
  f. ex-er-cise
  g. ex-ter-mi-nate
  h. fi-nal-ize
  i. fi-nance
  j. hy-phen-ate
  k. il-lu-mi-nate
  l. in-dus-tri-al
  m. jus-ti-fy
  n. le-gal-ize
  o. leg-is-late
  p. le-git-i-mize
  q. med-i-tate
  r. min-i-mize
  s. mu-ti-late
  t. sit-u-ate
  u. sum-ma-rize
  v. su-per-vise
  w. tan-ta-lize
  x. ter-ror-ize
  y. vis-u-al-ize

2.68 Can you visualize what the new room will look like?

2.69 Did he tantalize the dog until it bit him?

2.70 They will dramatize the story of Joseph.

2.71 We will finalize the instructions this afternoon.

2.72 Some people are working against the effort to legalize certain misdemeanors.

2.73 You should never terrorize anyone.

2.74 Will he finance your expedition?

2.75 They were trying to civilize the natives.

SELF TEST 2

2.01 d

2.02 e

2.03 a

2.04 c

2.05 g

2.06 j

2.07 i

2.08 f

2.09 a. Cocky

b. under the table

2.010 young men for factory work

2.011 looked Jewish

2.012 kill an informer

2.013 pray for the man

2.014 Corrie's

2.015 nonfiction

2.016 fiction

2.017 foreshadowing

2.018 flashback

2.019 Any order:

a. physical features

b. conduct

c. outward appearance

2.020 Any order:

a. actions

b. behavior

c. personality traits

2.021 Any order:

a. speak plainly

b. use relevant and to-the-point comments

c. don't use too much time

or disagree courteously, never hurt another person, never concentrate all attention on oneself

2.022 The alarm was sounded, and the Jews entered the hiding place with Corrie's help. The soldiers questioned the ten Booms, captured their visitors, and placed thirty-five under arrest. The Beje had been used as a trap.

2.023 Corrie's father cared very much for everyone—but especially for his children. He was willing to spend time with them and since he constantly read the Bible and prayed and relied on God—God gave him wisdom.

2.024 Yes, because when they kept their relationship with God right through daily fellowship, then they were ready for His leading and willing to do whatever He wanted.

2.025 It was in Corrie's bedroom. Another brick wall was added 30" in from the old one. It was aged and old bookshelves were put in front of the small opening.

SECTION 3

3.1 bus
3.2 promise not to cause any more trouble
3.3 open his door to anyone in need
3.4 Scheveningen
3.5 "God be with you"
3.6 watery, grey porridge
3.7 prison boredom
3.8 Any order:
  a. a Bible
  b. a needle and thread
  c. a toothbrush
  d. soap
3.9 bread only; no hot food; a punishment
3.10 scratching a calendar on the wall
3.11 when guards were away (they were celebrating Hitler's birthday)
3.12 all the Jews in the hiding place have escaped
3.13 She was put into a solitary cell because she was ill with a disease that she might give her cell mates; this punishment is worse because humans have social needs—we need to share and to listen and to see other people.
3.14 She took it apart and used the threads to embroider pictures on her pajamas.
3.15 An ant that came to eat any crumbs she dropped.
3.16 "March 9, 1944, Father. Released." was scratched on her wall calendar.
3.17 c
3.18 d
3.19 e
3.20 f
3.21 A Dutch police officer, who was Corrie's friend, had duty one night on their block, and allowed them to escape.
3.22 The mats were rolled up and put on end, coats were hung up with the arms draped over the one next to it. All personal articles were attractively arranged.
3.23 true
3.24 true
3.25 false
3.26 true
3.27 false
3.28 Thirty or forty people were placed in a railroad car; then that many more were packed into the small space. The train was attacked. The sisters could hear the machine guns and the bullets hitting the car.

3.29 Example:
The prisoners crawled out of the car, drank water eagerly from the lake, and marched over a mile to the prison. There they were allowed to rest awhile on lice infested straw. They spent the night exposed to rain and cold.
3.30 Corrie was able to conceal a sweater and her four copies of the Gospel under her dress. The woman in front of her was searched three times, and Betsie was searched, too.
3.31 Betsie had established a loving and trusting relationship with the Lord and had built upon it for many years. Therefore, she trusted Him whatever happened to her.
3.32 "For there lay Betsie ... had ministered to her."
3.33 "And so I ... hope of heaven."
3.34 Betsie looked radiantly young and happy and peaceful. All the weariness and pain had been erased from her face.
3.35 She was bewildered by the speed with which she was discharged. She could not believe it. She imagined all kinds of things going wrong, but no one stopped her.
3.36 "Even as the angry ... and so I discovered ... the love itself."
At first she was angry and vengeful but then she realized that Christ had died for everyone.
She was able to shake his hand only when God gave her His forgiveness and love.
3.37 Teacher check
3.38 biography
3.39 autobiography
3.40 Any order:
  a. to entertain
  b. to convince
  or persuade
  c. to expose something
  d. to incite to action
  e. to explain something
3.41 Any order:
  a. narration
  b. description
  c. exposition
  d. persuasion
3.42 *-tion, -sion,* and *-ity*
3.43 nouns
3.44 repeat
3.45 ascend
3.46 imagine
3.47 justify
3.48 describe

3.49 illustrate
3.50 substitute
3.51 create
3.52 institute
3.53 Any order:
  a. just
  b. tan
  c. on
  d. in
  e. sit
  f. cat
  g. no
  h. fiction
  i. it
  j. if
  k. not
  l. citation
  m. ton
  n. sat
  o. is
  or son, us
3.54 a. fission
  b. cavity
  c. brevity
  d. detention
  e. submission
3.55 petition
3.56 levity
3.57 pension
3.58 Ascension
3.59 denomination
3.60 ammunition
3.61 gravity
3.62 hypertension
3.63 extension
3.64 fission
3.65 permission
3.66 institution
3.67 superstition

SELF TEST 3

3.01 j
3.02 i
3.03 d
3.04 f
3.05 c
3.06 g
3.07 e
3.08 k
3.09 a
3.010 l
3.011 Any order:
  a. to entertain
  b. to convince
  or persuade
  c. to explain
  d. to expose something
  e. to invite to action
3.012 Any order:
  a. speaking plainly
  b. concentrating
  c. not using too much time
3.013 behavior *or* conduct
3.014 make the part defective
3.015 the underground
3.016 razzia
3.017 the Gestapo
3.018 On Hitler's birthday, the guards left their posts. The prisoners passed messages along to each other.
3.019 Betsie's expression in death revealed peace and happiness. She had escaped imprisonment.
3.020 She brings God's Word to the prisoners. Not only does she encourage them, she helps them physically. She also witnesses to the enemy whenever possible.

LIFEPAC TEST

1. i
2. h
3. b
4. a
5. g
6. j
7. k
8. c
9. d
10. e
11. c
12. c
13. d
14. a
15. b
16. a
17. Examples; any order:
   a. honesty
   b. kindness
   c. loyalty
   or unselfishness, goodness
18. speed
19. underground
20. Gestapo
21. speaking plainly
22. behavior
   or conduct
23. A Dutch police officer, who was Corrie's friend, had duty one night on their block and allowed them to escape.
24. Betsie had established a loving and trusting relationship with the Lord and had built upon it for many years. Therefore, she trusted Him no matter what happened to her.
25. She set out to speak to others about her experience and faith. She even went to Germany to work with her former enemies.

ALTERNATE LIFEPAC TEST

1. h
2. e
3. i
4. c
5. k
6. a
7. g
8. j
9. f
10. d
11. true
12. false
13. false
14. true
15. a. 1
   b. 5
   c. 3
   d. 2
   e. 4
16. a. Peter
   b. played Wilhelmus (Dutch national anthem)
17. cruelty
18. Any order:
   a. reading
   b. listening
   c. speaking
19. a. died
   b. been released
   or had begun helping spread Christianity and forgiveness among the Germans
20. a
21. c
22. b
23. Example:
   Corrie was able to carry out God's purpose by her strength of character. She provided for the persecuted Jews and smuggled in the Gospels. She grew as a Christian and was finally able to forgive her persecutors and help them find Christ.
24. Example:
   Betsie was unquestioningly faithful and accepting. She always spread messages of God's love for all. She died in the knowledge that she was going to a better place.
25. Example:
   A character sketch should express the author's personal opinion about his subject. It may deal with one or several personality traits. If the writer outlines his subject to plan the main ideas and supporting details he uses, the paper will be better organized. Always proofread and correct any mistakes.

SPELLING TEST

1	circumference	David's statue had a **circumference** of four feet.	circumference
2	reliance	Paul's **reliance** was in the Lord.	reliance
3	acceptance	It is natural to seek **acceptance** from our friends.	acceptance
4	exuberance	Dawn's friends loved her **exuberance**.	exuberance
5	concordance	The students worked on the project in perfect **concordance**.	concordance
6	allowance	Greg's teacher made an **allowance** for his tardiness.	allowance
7	alliance	The two friends share a strong **alliance**.	alliance
8	brilliance	The stars shone with unusual **brilliance** last night.	brilliance
9	loveliness	Each child has a **loveliness** all its own.	loveliness
10	blessedness	The Pastor spoke about the quality of **blessedness**.	blessedness
11	resistance	Jim's **resistance** to temptation was rewarded.	resistance
12	hindrance	Ann's handicap was not a **hindrance** to her love of sports.	hindrance
13	effectiveness	His speech lost its **effectiveness** at the end.	effectiveness
14	greatness	Jesus' apostles had a mark of **greatness**.	greatness
15	analyze	He would **analyze** each report slowly.	analyze
16	create	Let's work to **create** an atmosphere of love.	create
17	exercise	We all need daily **exercise** to keep our bodies healthy.	exercise
18	finalize	Please **finalize** your statement.	finalize
19	hyphenate	I have a list of words for you to **hyphenate**.	hyphenate
20	justify	John tried to **justify** his actions with words.	justify
21	legalize	His lawyer sought to **legalize** the agreement.	legalize
22	legitimize	Our law officers try not to **legitimize** violence.	legitimize
23	meditate	Ann likes to **meditate** on the Bible each morning.	meditate
24	mutilate	Another rain storm will **mutilate** the garden.	mutilate
25	summarize	I would like to **summarize** what I've read.	summarize
26	tantalize	The buffet was prepared to **tantalize** the guests.	tantalize

SPELLING TEST

27	visualize	Susan could not **visualize** the problem.	visualize
28	repetition	**Repetition** of musical sounds makes a melody.	repetition
29	petition	The voters wrote up a **petition** to eliminate the law.	petition
30	ascension	Jesus' **ascension** into heaven took place at Bethany.	ascension
31	denomination	Each **denomination** was represented.	denomination
32	justification	No **justification** was needed to prove his abilities.	justification
33	description	Please write a **description** of how you feel.	description
34	levity	A little **levity** helps to relax everyone.	levity
35	permission	You do not need my **permission** to stay home.	permission
36	substitution	Gene was a good **substitution** on the team.	substitution
37	pension	Some companies provide a **pension** for their retired employees.	pension
38	fission	Nuclear **fission** is a reaction that releases massive amounts of energy when atoms split.	fission
39	hypertension	My child has a problem with **hypertension**.	hypertension
40	cavity	A cave is a natural **cavity** in the earth.	cavity

LANGUAGE ARTS 707

ALTERNATE LIFEPAC TEST

NAME _____

DATE _____

SCORE _____

Match these items (each answer, 2 points).

1. _____ Gestapo
2. _____ underground
3. _____ flashback
4. _____ foreshadowing
5. _____ razzia
6. _____ Beje
7. _____ Ravensbruck
8. _____ biography
9. _____ autobiography
10. _____ Holland

a. the ten Boom's house

b. imaginative prose

c. a hint of a future even

d. occupied by the Nazis

e. a secret group organized to oppose occupation forces

f. an account of actual events experienced by the author

g. A German prison for Jews and prisoners of war

h. secret police force of the German Nazis

i. the telling of an event that happened at a previous time

j. written account of an actual person's life

k. lightning raids by the Nazis searching for factory workers

Answer *true* or *false* (each answer, 1 point).

11. _____ *Narration* is a type of writing telling what happened; it describes an event or a series of events.

12. _____ Descriptive writing, consisting of vivid and clear details, is primarily used to incite the reader to action.

13. _____ Exposition is used to appeal to the senses rather than to logic and reason.

14. _____ Propaganda is frequently used by newspaper writers.

Number these events in chronological sequence (each answer, 2 points).

15. a. _____ Holland is occupied by German forces.

    b. _____ Corrie is able to forgive her Nazi guard.

    c. _____ The ten Booms are captured in a raid.

    d. _____ The hiding place is built.

    e. _____ Betsie becomes ill.

Complete these sentences (each answer, 3 points).

16. Corrie's nephew a. _____ was arrested because he b. _____

    _____ .

17. A young German named Otto showed the personality trait of _____ in his behavior toward Christoffels.

18. A person needs to be able to determine main ideas and essential details when he is

    a. _____ , b. _____ , or c. _____ .

19. By the end of the story Betsie and her father had a. _____ and Corrie had

    b. _____ .

Write the letter for the correct answer on each line (each answer, 2 points).

20. While imprisoned in Scheveningen, Corrie is able to _____ .
    a. witness to her interrogator
    b. work in a hospital
    c. stay with Betsie
    d. be with her father

21. Which statement is *not* true as a result of the raid? _____
    a. The ten Booms were imprisoned.
    b. Ten days after his arrest Mr. Ten Boom died.
    c. The Jews hidden by the ten Booms were captured.
    d. Corrie was placed in a solitary cell because of her illness.

22. The *incorrectly* spelled word is _____ .
    a. terrorize   b. discription
    c. detention   d. exterminate

Complete these activities (each answer, 5 points).

23. Explain the importance of Christian faith in Corrie's life.

    _____
    _____
    _____
    _____

24. How did Betsie's life reflect Christianity?

    _____
    _____
    _____
    _____

25. Describe the way to write a character sketch.

    _____
    _____
    _____
    _____

ALTERNATE SPELLING TEST

1	dependence	They had a mutual **dependence** on each other.	dependence
2	insurance	Jesus' word is our **insurance**.	insurance
3	residence	The Martin family moved their **residence** to Florida.	residence
4	exuberance	Dawn's friends loved her **exuberance**.	exuberance
5	credence	A Christian's **credence** in the Bible is necessary.	credence
6	concordance	The students worked on the project in perfect **concordance**.	concordance
7	nuisance	Lisa's bad humor became a **nuisance** to the class.	nuisance
8	compliance	We should always live in **compliance** with God's will.	compliance
9	patience	Let's practice **patience** with each other.	patience
10	loveliness	Each child has a **loveliness** all its own.	loveliness
11	gratitude	Mary's **gratitude** to her mother was tremendous.	gratitude
12	blessedness	The Pastor spoke about the quality of **blessedness**.	blessedness
13	musician	We were grateful for the **musician** in church Sunday.	musician
14	intelligence	Many years of work and study developed the scholar's **intelligence**.	intelligence
15	effectiveness	His speech lost its **effectiveness** at the end.	effectiveness
16	civilize	The missionaries' goal was to **civilize** the tribe.	civilize
17	cremate	In some cultures people **cremate** their dead.	cremate
18	dramatize	Linda's assignment was to **dramatize** her work.	dramatize
19	exercise	We all need daily **exercise** to keep our bodies healthy.	exercise
20	exterminate	The farmer sprayed his crops to **exterminate** the insects.	exterminate
21	finance	Gary's family helped **finance** his education.	finance
22	industrial	Christopher's father worked in an **industrial** complex.	industrial
23	legislate	It's the responsibility of Congress to **legislate** the law.	legislate
24	illuminate	Most evenings the moon will **illuminate** our atmosphere.	illuminate
25	minimize	She tried to **minimize** her boredom by reading a book.	minimize
26	situate	The runner had to **situate** himself on the starting line.	situate

ALTERNATE SPELLING TEST

27	supervise	Mr. Collins was asked to **supervise** their activities.	supervise
28	terrorize	Kidnappers often **terrorize** their victims.	terrorize
29	submission	His wife's attitude was one of **submission**.	submission
30	imagination	How much do you use your **imagination**?	imagination
31	detention	The juvenile was kept in **detention** until his parents were notified.	detention
32	illustration	The artist drew a beautiful **illustration**.	illustration
33	description	Please write a **description** of how you feel.	description
34	ammunition	The hunters were asked to bring their own **ammunition**.	ammunition
35	institution	School is one type of **institution**.	institution
36	extension	He had several days **extension** to finish the project.	extension
37	superstition	Don't let a **superstition** distort the facts.	superstition
38	creation	The world is God's **creation**.	creation
39	gravity	We are able to walk due to the earth's **gravity**.	gravity
40	levity	Bob interjected **levity** into the serious discussion.	levity

LANGUAGE ARTS 708

Unit 8: Literature

TEACHER NOTES

MATERIALS NEEDED FOR LIFEPAC	
Required	Suggested
None	• King James Version of the Bible • dictionary • a short story or article • a book about Native American sign language • reference books or online sources

ADDITIONAL LEARNING ACTIVITIES

Section 1: Learning About Nonfiction Literature

1. Choose another biography or autobiography and read excerpts to the students. Discuss key events and characters involved.

2. Choose a person from the Bible. Discuss his or her character traits. Are they described or revealed through actions?

3. Discuss the key events in Christ's life.

4. Extended Writing Assignment: Write a nonfiction (biographical or autobiographical) account using conversation, key events, several characters, and sequence of events.
    Write about a meaningful, humorous, exciting, embarrassing, or disappointing experience. Check the first section if you have any problems. Remember to use commas and semicolons correctly.

Section 2: Learning to Listen

1. Read the students the directions for doing some project. It may be a sketch, diagram, or other type of activity.

2. Ask students to describe a process to the class. Are the directions clear? Have the students summarize these directions.

3. Bring to class a short story or article detailing information. Read this article to a small group and have them point out the important ideas. Write a summary from these ideas. See if the summary covers all the information.

4. Listen to a religious, historical, or news program. Write a summary of this program.

Section 3: Speaking With Gestures

1. Write several simple messages or feelings on different pieces of paper. Ask a student to select one and use gestures to convey the meaning.

2. Plan a message or quotation. "Send" it to another group using sign language.

3. Plan and present your own pantomime to the students.

Administer the LIFEPAC Spelling Test.

The test is provided in this Teacher's Guide.

Evaluate the tests and review the words the students spelled incorrectly.

If necessary, review all of the words in the unit to prepare for the alternate spelling test.

Administer the Alternate LIFEPAC Spelling test that is provided in this Teacher's Guide.

Administer the LIFEPAC Test.

The test is to be administered in one session. Give no help except with directions.

Evaluate the tests and review areas where the students have done poorly.

Review the pages and activities that stress the concepts tested.

If necessary, administer the Alternate LIFEPAC Test.

ANSWER KEYS

SECTION 1

1.1   F

1.2   N

1.3   N

1.4   F

1.5   N

1.6   N

1.7   F

1.8   N

1.9   *nonfiction –*
factual literature dealing with truth or reality

1.10 *fiction –*
imaginative literature

1.11 false

1.12 false

1.13 true

1.14 false

1.15 true

1.16   a. The story took place when Helen was nearly seven years of age.
   b. The story took place at the home of Helen Keller.
   c. Helen's mother, Miss Anne Sullivan, and Helen Keller
   d. Helen Keller's mother engaged the best teacher she could find for Helen and prepared a room for her so that Helen could be taught at home. Helen learned to imitate the letters of words Miss Sullivan wrote in the palm of Helen's hand. When she could not understand the meanings of these words, Helen became frustrated and broke the doll Miss Sullivan had given her. Miss Sullivan took her to the pump house. Helen Keller's hand was placed under the running water as Miss Sullivan spelled w-a-t-e-r in the other palm. The mystery language was revealed to Helen.
   e. Her entire life was changed. Helen discovered that the light of knowledge had replaced darkness, joy had replaced anger and bitterness, hope had replaced dejection, and joyful anticipation had replaced gloom and sadness. She was able to understand that everything has a name. She realized that order and meaning did exist in the world and that she had found the key.

1.17   a. when
   b. where
   c. who
   d. what
   e. results

1.18 factual

1.19 *to involve* or *to be involved*

1.20 the important things that happen, the events which unlock the meaning of a story

1.21 Miss Anne Sullivan

1.22 fifty

1.23 vibrations of sound in the throat

1.24 Example:
Anne Sullivan patiently taught her to communicate with the outside world. In the process she gave her love and confidence. Helen Keller graduated from college and began to work for legislation for the blind. She wrote many books and encouraged millions of handicapped people.

1.25 Example:
He may be physically blind or he may be spiritually blind. Although physical blindness cannot always be healed, spiritual blindness disappears when one receives Jesus as his Savior.

1.26 a

1.27 b

1.28 b

1.29 b

1.30 b

1.31 a

1.32 b

1.33 a

1.34 a

1.35 b

1.36 b

1.37 a

1.38 Example:
The story took place shortly after the death of the author's mother.

1.39 Example:
The story took place in a grocery store.

1.40 Any order:
   a. the author
   b. the woman
   c. the woman's son
   d. the owner of the store
   e. the author's mother
   or the neighbor, Mrs. Jones

1.41   Example:
I became very much interested in Junior's gobbling peanuts like a turkey eating grasshoppers and throwing the shells on the floor. I am interested in him because I would like to teach him some manners and show him God's love and help him understand the moral law.

1.42   Any order:
   a. worship false gods
   b. making graven images
   c. taking God's name in vain
   d. dishonor father and mother
   e. kill
   f. commit adultery
   or covet a neighbor's possession, bear false witness

1.43   footsteps,

1.44   C

1.45   IC

1.46   I did not know that I was spelling a word; I was simply making my fingers go in a monkey-like imitation.

1.47   I learned a great many new words that day; however, I do not remember what they all were.

1.48   I do not remember what they all were; but I do remember that *mother*, *father*, *sister*, and *teacher* were among them.

1.49   Their homes were in Great Falls, Montana; Cedar Falls, Iowa; and Falls Church, Virginia.

1.50   a. appearance
   b. appreciate
   c. appropriate
   d. communication
   e. demonstrate
   f. effectively
   g. emphasis
   h. entertainment
   i. experience
   j. factual
   k. gestures
   l. impatience
   m. involved
   n. legislative
   o. logical
   p. monetary
   q. mourning
   r. opportunity
   s. organization
   t. penetrated
   u. persisted
   v. repentance
   w. sequence
   x. spiritual
   y. urgent

1.51   Sentences will vary.
Examples:
   a. *appearance* –
      He gave the appearance of being happy.
   b. *appreciate* –
      They appreciate all that you have done for them.
   c. *appropriate* –
      Jane always wears appropriate clothes for every occasion.
   d. *communication* –
      Communication is essential to maintain good understanding of the situation.
   e. *demonstrate* –
      Demonstrate brotherly love.
   f. *effectively* –
      The speaker presented his ideas effectively.
   g. *emphasis* –
      The curriculum puts emphasis on developing the whole person.
   h. *entertainment* –
      Entertainment was provided for the children.
   i. *experience* –
      Jennifer said, "My greatest experience was when I came to know Jesus!"
   j. *factual* –
      Gregg prefers factual stories.
   k. *gestures* –
      Your gestures often speak louder than your words.
   l. *impatience* –
      He manifested his impatience.
   m. *involved* –
      Jane became deeply involved in volunteer work.
   n. *legislative* –
      The legislative department has the duty and the power to make the laws.
   o. *logical* –
      He explained the events in logical order.
   p. *monetary* –
      They presented the hero with a monetary reward.
   q. *mourning* –
      He turns our mourning into joy.
   r. *opportunity* –
      Although Gale had the opportunity to go to Europe, she chose to stay home.
   s. *organization* –
      Organization is essential to good writing.

t. *penetrated* –
The light penetrated the darkness.
u. *persisted* –
His cough persisted for months.
v. *repentance* –
Repentance means being sorry enough
for wrong doing to give it up.
w. *sequence* –
The words are arranged in alphabetical
sequence.
x. *spiritual* –
Spiritual sight brings understanding of
the Bible.
y. *urgent* –
He received an urgent message to call
home at once.
— Teacher check

SELF TEST 1

1.01 d
1.02 h
1.03 i
1.04 k
1.05 a
1.06 j
1.07 c
1.08 e
1.09 a. factual
b. imaginative
1.010 providing her with an outstanding teacher
1.011 important things that happen that unlock the meaning
1.012 a. seven
b. Miss Anne Sullivan
1.013 flashbacks
1.014 Any order:
a. when
b. where
c. who
d. what
1.015 involved
1.016 false
1.017 true
1.018 true
1.019 false
1.020 true
1.021 false
1.022 false
1.023 true
1.024 Example:
Her arrival marked a new part of Helen
Keller's life. She had a loving companion and
teacher to help her.
1.025 Example:
Helen Keller realized that all things had
names. She recognized order and logic in the
world. It changed her life. She could learn to
communicate, and she had a new attitude
toward life.
1.026 Example:
He was grateful because she had taught him
the moral law when he was young.
or
She was not afraid to punish him when he
disobeyed the moral law.

SECTION 2

2.1   a. *listen* –
       to try to hear, attend closely with the ears
       b. *hear* –
       to perceive by ear

2.2   Any order:
       a. daydreaming about personal achievements
       b. thinking about family problems
       c. feeling angry toward someone
       d. thinking about exciting plans

2.3   Either order:
       a. courteous listening (pay attention)
       b. note taking

2.4   Write key words, not every word the speaker says; discover word meaning by usage; arrange ideas in proper order.

2.5   a. recall
       b. main
       c. key

2.6   a. to unlock
       b. to enable you to easily recall the main ideas

2.7   new words

2.8   proper sequence
       or order

2.9   Teacher check

2.10   Any order:
       a. What is the problem or issue?
       b. What are the most important supporting ideas?
       c. What was the conclusion or decision made?

2.11   Teacher check

2.12   Summary checking guidelines.
       a. X
       b. X
       c. X
       d. X

2.13   Teacher check

2.14   a. ri - ot - ous
       b. taking part in a riot; boisterous; disorderly

2.15   a. e - mo - tion- al
       b. of the emotions; showing emotions; appealing to the emotions

2.16   a. as - sump - tion
       b. taking for granted; supposing

2.17   a. com - pre - hend
       b. understand meaning of

2.18   a. as - cer - tain
       b. find out; determine

2.19   b
2.20   b
2.21   c
2.22   c
2.23   b
2.24   b
2.25   a
2.26   b
2.27   b
2.28   a

2.29-2.38   Sentences will vary.
       Examples:

2.29   *conclusion* –
       After his experience he reached the conclusion that doing the right thing is always better.

2.30   *breathtaking* –
       His experience was breathtaking.

2.31   *independent* –
       Often one with an independent spirit has not learned obedience or submission.

2.32   *devoted* –
       The mother devoted all of her time to the care of her children.

2.33   *forgiveness* –
       Forgiveness brings love and healing.

2.34   *graciously* –
       She graciously opened her home to the homeless.

2.35   *harmonious* –
       The family worked and played together as a harmonious group.

2.36   *instructor* –
       Miss Jones is a good instructor.

2.37   *summarize* –
       You have learned to summarize well.

2.38   *unassuming* –
       Although she is quite accomplished, she is very unassuming.

       — Teacher check

SELF TEST 2

2.01 c
2.02 b
2.03 e
2.04 d
2.05 f
2.06 a
2.07 Any order:
a. what was the main issue or problem
b. what were the important supporting ideas
c. what was the conclusion or decision
2.08 Either order:
a. courteous listening
b. note taking
2.09 Any order:
a. daydreaming
b. worrying
c. anger
2.010 a. Helen Keller
b. Anne Sullivan
2.011 a. pump house
b. everything had a name
2.012 flashback
2.013 a. brick
b. apple tree switch
c. return the brick
d. apologize
2.014 Example:
I can show courtesy to a speaker by listening quietly and attentively and by looking at him when I am not taking notes.
2.015 Any order:
a. Have I included the main ideas in my topic sentence?
b. Is my summary one-third or one-fourth as long as the original?
c. Have I given the speaker's or author's opinion in my own words?
d. Is the summary clear and concise?

SECTION 3

3.1 extend the meaning of their words
3.2 Any order:
a. too many are used
b. they are unsuitable
c. the speaker has nervous habits
3.3 poised
3.4 use appropriate gestures
3.5 a. *gesture* –
using motions of body or limbs
b. *universal* –
applying to everyone or existing everywhere
3.6 Examples; any order:
a. shrug shoulders
b. clenched fist
c. arms stretched out—palms up
d. point with forefinger
e. hand(s)
3.7 Any order:
a. hand on heart for pledge of allegiance
b. head bowed in prayer
c. patting another on the back
d. waving or shaking hands
e. nodding or shaking the head
3.8 Either order:
a. to communicate
b. to entertain
3.9 Either order:
a. Native American tribes
b. the deaf
3.10 Any order:
a. shaking or nodding the head
b. forefinger to lips
c. index finger on the temple
or scratch head, beckon, wave to come, hold hand out to stop
3.11 Teacher check
3.12 Teacher check
3.13 false
3.14 true
3.15 true
3.16 a play without words in which gestures or actions express the meaning
3.17 Teacher check
3.18 c
3.19 e
3.20 a
3.21 b

3.22-3.25 Sentences will vary.
Examples:

3.22 Using colorful words you may *portray* the beauty of a sunset.

3.23 It is difficult to *depict* a scene that you have not seen.

3.24 The teacher has *authority* in the classroom.

3.25 He showed his *defiance* by refusing to obey regulations.

	Correct spelling		Rule
3.26	a. advising	b.	A
3.27	a. advertising	b.	A
3.28	a. appropriating	b.	A
3.29	a. arguing	b.	A
3.30	a. arrangement	b.	D
3.31	a. becoming	b.	A
3.32	a. changeable	b.	B
3.33	a. communicating	b.	A
3.34	a. dining	b.	A
3.35	a. dyeing	b.	C
3.36	a. elated	b.	A
3.37	a. extremely	b.	D
3.38	a. excitement	b.	D
3.39	a. fascinating	b.	A
3.40	a. gabbling	b.	A
3.41	a. graceless	b.	D
3.42	a. imagined	b.	A
3.43	a. management	b.	D
3.44	a. persuading	b.	A
3.45	a. resourceful	b.	D

SELF TEST 3

3.01 i

3.02 h

3.03 g

3.04 d

3.05 c

3.06 l

3.07 j

3.08 f

3.09 e

3.10 Either order:
a. using gestures or signs
b. spelling words in the deaf alphabet

3.011 factual

3.012 Either order:
a. Greeks
b. Romans

3.013 sequence

3.014 topic

3.015 sign language

3.016 too loud

3.017 words

3.018 true

3.019 true

3.020 false

3.021 false

3.022 true

3.023 true

3.024 false

3.025 false

3.026 false

3.027 true

3.028 true

3.029 true

3.030 Examples:
a. *pantomime* –
plays without words, using gestures to entertain or amuse
b. *gesture* –
the use of motions of the body to communicate thoughts or ideas
c. *universal* –
applying to everyone or existing everywhere
d. *flashback* –
going back to an event at an earlier time; retrospective

LIFEPAC TEST

1. d
2. n
3. f
4. m
5. j
6. l
7. b
8. e
9. i
10. h
11. k
12. a
13. Either order:
    a. blind
    b. deaf
14. speak
15. summarized
16. fiction
17. Either order:
    a. courtesy
    b. taking notes
18. gestures
19. pantomime *or* mime
20. intensify
21. Any order:
    a. recall details
    b. recognize main ideas
    c. record key words
22. Either order:
    a. signals *or* gestures
    b. spelling words in the deaf alphabet
23. Any order:
    a. What was the main issue?
    b. What were important details?
    c. What was the conclusion?
24. Examples; any order:
    a. nod or shake head
    b. wave or shake hands
    c. hand out for stop
    or beckon for come

ALTERNATE LIFEPAC TEST

1. c
2. i
3. k
4. a
5. e
6. f
7. b
8. g
9. j
10. h
11. Any order:
    a. what was the main problem
    b. what were the most important supporting ideas
    c. what is the conclusion or decision made
12. Examples; any order:
    a. a topic sentence expressing the main idea
    b. a length of about one-fourth to one-third the original
    c. an expression of the original ideas, not the student's
13. Either order:
    a. communication
    b. entertainment
14. Either order:
    a. Native American
    b. the deaf
15. true
16. false
17. false
18. true
19. true
20. true
21. Examples; any order:
    a. daydreaming
    b. worrying or problems
    c. anger or excitement

SPELLING TEST

1	advancement	The swift **advancement** of the snowstorm caught everyone by surprise.	advancement
2	advertisement	The apple pie **advertisement** in the magazine aroused my taste buds.	advertisement
3	argument	The **argument** subsided when no one could remember the initial issue.	argument
4	authority	As Christians, we see the absolute **authority** of God.	authority
5	changeable	The man's fishing story was as **changeable** as the wind.	changeable
6	defiance	Utter **defiance** could be seen in the lion's eyes as the hunter came face to face with his prey.	defiance
7	dining	The **dining** area was adjacent to the dining room.	dining
8	elated	Vicki was **elated** after playing her first game of racquetball.	elated
9	excitement	Danelle could not contain her **excitement**.	excitement
10	gabbled	The little girl **gabbled** on and on, but no one could understand a word she said.	gabbled
11	imagined	Billy **imagined** he was a knight of the realm as he sat on his pony.	imagined
12	management	The **management** was happy at the turnout for the Grand Opening.	management
13	persuading	Children can be very **persuading** when they want to be.	persuading
14	resourceful	The **resourceful** hiker carried an extra pair of shoes on the trip.	resourceful
15	appearance	The **appearance** of the wolf startled the sheep.	appearance
16	appreciate	I **appreciate** all the help you have given me.	appreciate
17	communication	A lack of **communication** between children and their parents can lead to problems.	communication
18	effectively	The weatherman **effectively** predicted the weekend weather.	effectively
19	entertainment	The pastor played his musical saw at the talent show, which was much to our **entertainment**.	entertainment
20	factual	The book I read was a **factual** account of a plane crash in Alaska.	factual
21	impatience	The children's **impatience** to depart for the zoo was evident.	impatience

SPELLING TEST

22	legislative	The **legislative** branch of our government makes the laws.	legislative
23	monetary	The **monetary** system which we use today replaced the barter system.	monetary
24	opportunity	We should use every **opportunity** presented to share our Father's love.	opportunity
25	penetrated	During our hiking trip, we **penetrated** deep into the forest.	penetrated
26	repentance	Upon **repentance**, a warm, secure contentment came over me.	repentance
27	spiritual	God wants us to take care of our **spiritual** bodies as well as our physical bodies.	spiritual
28	ascertain	It was difficult at the accident scene to **ascertain** who was in the wrong.	ascertain
29	assumption	Sometimes a quick **assumption** can lead to an incorrect conclusion.	assumption
30	burdensome	Christ promises His children that His yoke is not **burdensome**.	burdensome
31	conclusion	After the **conclusion** of the debate, everyone was much more relaxed.	conclusion
32	emotional	**Emotional** good-byes were said as Elizabeth left for college.	emotional
33	forefathers	One of my **forefathers** was the bodyguard to George Washington.	forefathers
34	foreman	The construction **foreman** hired two additional men for the new site.	foreman
35	forethought	Good devotions require **forethought**.	forethought
36	forgiveness	God's **forgiveness** of our sins shows just how caring He is to His children.	forgiveness
37	graciously	The hostess **graciously** thanked her guests for attending.	graciously
38	independent	The **independent** boy completed his project without anyone's help.	independent
39	riotous	The **riotous** demonstration did not achieve its purpose.	riotous
40	unassuming	The new pastor of the church was **unassuming**.	unassuming

LANGUAGE ARTS 708

ALTERNATE LIFEPAC TEST

NAME _____

DATE _____

SCORE _____

52 / 65

Match these items (each answer, 2 points).

1. _____ pantomime
2. _____ gesture
3. _____ key events
4. _____ summarize
5. _____ Junior
6. _____ Annie Sullivan
7. _____ Helen Keller
8. _____ Harold Dye
9. _____ nonfiction
10. _____ fiction

a. to rewrite main ideas in shortened form

b. a determined, stubborn person who overcame personal handicaps

c. a play without words

d. a problem in listening

e. a spoiled person who did not learn a lesson in the story

f. a person who helped another devotedly

g. a person who learned a lesson and wanted to pass it along

h. imaginative writing

i. any bodily movement having meaning

j. a true account

k. meaningful happenings

Complete these sentences (each answer, 3 points).

11. To make a brief summary you should answer three questions:

    a. _____ ,

    b. _____ and ,

    c. _____ .

12. Four things to check a summary for include clarity and conciseness,

    a. _____ ,

    b. _____ and ,

    c. _____ .

13. Two functions of gestures are a. _____ and b. _____ .

14. Two groups of people using gestures are a. _____ and

    b. _____ .

Answer *true* **or** *false* (each answer, 1 point).

15. _____ Shrugging the shoulders is a gesture universally showing indifference or puzzlement.

16. _____ Gestures are always used instead of words.

17. _____ A person might beckon to tell another to go away.

18. _____ The word *changeable* is spelled correctly.

19. _____ The word *riotous* is spelled correctly.

20. _____ Effective listening includes courteous listening and note taking.

Complete this activity (each answer, 3 points).

21. List three problems students may have in listening.

    a. _____

    b. _____

    c. _____

ALTERNATE SPELLING TEST

1	advising	After **advising** his friend, Rob had second thoughts.	advising
2	advancement	The swift **advancement** of the snowstorm caught everyone by surprise.	advancement
3	appropriating	The treasurer has taken care of **appropriating** the necessary funds.	appropriating
4	arguing	**Arguing** is not the best way to settle the matter.	arguing
5	becoming	Patti's new haircut was most **becoming**.	becoming
6	communicating	**Communicating** is a good way to learn about the people around us.	communicating
7	depict	The painting will **depict** the true lifestyle of the early settlers.	depict
8	dyeing	Katrina is **dyeing** the cloth before she begins sewing it.	dyeing
9	extremely	After he fell in, Bob found that the creek was **extremely** cold.	extremely
10	fascinating	The undersea world is a **fascinating** part of God's creation.	fascinating
11	graceless	The **graceless** rhinoceros was seen floundering about in the high brush.	graceless
12	management	The **management** was happy at the turnout for the Grand Opening.	management
13	portray	Benjamin will **portray** Joseph in the Christmas pageant.	portray
14	appearance	The **appearance** of the wolf startled the sheep.	appearance
15	appropriate	Judy did not have an **appropriate** outfit for the affair.	appropriate
16	demonstrate	The choir will **demonstrate** their musical abilities at the spring concert.	demonstrate
17	emphasis	Many teenagers today realize that much **emphasis** is placed on peer pressure.	emphasis
18	experience	Mountain climbing requires practice and **experience**.	experience
19	gestures	A mime uses many **gestures**, including facial and body movements.	gestures
20	involved	Some people attend church while others get **involved** in church.	involved
21	logical	The procedure was not in a **logical** order.	logical

ALTERNATE SPELLING TEST

22	mourning	Jesus comforts people during their period of **mourning**.	mourning
23	organization	The **organization** of the picnic was excellent.	organization
24	persisted	Jim **persisted** in his efforts until help completed the project.	persisted
25	repentance	Upon **repentance**, a warm, secure contentment came over me.	repentance
26	sequence	The **sequence** in a mystery story is vital to the solution of the story itself.	sequence
27	urgent	There is an **urgent** phone call for you.	urgent
28	breathtaking	The view from the swinging bridge was utterly **breathtaking**.	breathtaking
29	burdensome	Christ promises His children that his yoke is not **burdensome**.	burdensome
30	comprehend	Although the Bible is sometimes difficult to **comprehend**, the Holy Spirit is always there to guide you.	comprehend
31	devoted	It is wonderful to have a family that is so **devoted** to one another.	devoted
32	forecast	The **forecast** for today was excellent, but the weather was not.	forecast
33	forehead	Bob received a nasty cut on his **forehead** while playing football today.	forehead
34	forerunner	John the Baptist was a **forerunner** to Jesus.	forerunner
35	foresight	It takes **foresight** to plan a college education.	foresight
36	forgiveness	God's **forgiveness** of our sins shows just how caring He is to His children.	forgiveness
37	harmonious	The **harmonious** melodies of the spring concert brought happiness to many.	harmonious
38	instructor	My painting **instructor** believes I have potential.	instructor
39	summarize	The last step in the debate will be to **summarize** your facts.	summarize
40	excitement	Danelle could not contain her **excitement**.	excitement

LANGUAGE ARTS 709

Unit 9: Compositions

TEACHER NOTES

MATERIALS NEEDED FOR LIFEPAC	
Required	Suggested
None	• King James Version of the Bible • a few approved books and magazines • dictionary • encyclopedia or biographical dictionary • a book of approved limericks • reference books or online sources

ADDITIONAL LEARNING ACTIVITIES

Section 1: Writing Sentences

1. Take some sentences from such nonsense literature as "Jabberwocky" and write on the board, or have students turn to that section in the LIFEPAC. Notice the types of sentences used. How can you tell which type each sentence is? You might see if students pick subjects (example: *toves*) and verbs (example: *gyre* and *gimble*).
    Ask, "How can you tell these words are subjects or verbs?"

2. Look in magazines and newspapers for examples of sentence errors.
    Compare examples with other groups.

3. Listen to a casual conversation. Record any sentence types or errors you hear.
    Do not embarrass anyone by revealing the source of this conversation.
    Notice that fragments are more frequently used in very casual conversation (example: *Yes!*).

Section 2: Writing Paragraphs

1. Select several paragraphs from various sources: Dickens, Twain, Poe, or magazine articles. Read sample paragraphs to the students (or duplicate the paragraphs on sheets of paper) and let the students detect the patterns of development and any paragraph flaws evident.

2. Look through various sources (books and magazines) for an example of each pattern of paragraph development you have studied. Write each example neatly on a separate page and see if another group can correctly identify each pattern.

3. Outline a paragraph written in any pattern.
    Does it have a topic sentence? unity? logical sequence?

Section 3: Pronouncing Words

1. Write several difficult to pronounce words on the board (example: *subtle, entente, entourage,* and so on). Ask students to pronounce these words.

2. Think of some qualities or objects that would necessitate "coining" words. Use your invented words in sentences and let another group see if they can determine the meanings of these words from context clues.

3. Find some unusual coined words and present them (with their meanings) to the students.

Administer the LIFEPAC Spelling Test.

The test is provided in this Teacher's Guide.

Evaluate the tests and review the words the students spelled incorrectly.

If necessary, review all of the words in the unit to prepare for the alternate spelling test.

Administer the Alternate LIFEPAC Spelling test that is provided in this Teacher's Guide.

Administer the LIFEPAC Test.

The test is to be administered in one session. Give no help except with directions.

Evaluate the tests and review areas where the students have done poorly.

Review the pages and activities that stress the concepts tested.

If necessary, administer the Alternate LIFEPAC Test.

ANSWER KEYS

SECTION 1

1.1 declarative
1.2 exclamatory
1.3 declarative
1.4 declarative
1.5 interrogative
1.6 declarative
1.7 interrogative
1.8 imperative
1.9 declarative
1.10 declarative
1.11 imperative
1.12 imperative
1.13 interrogative
1.14 imperative
1.15 declarative
1.16 declarative
1.17 exclamatory
1.18 declarative
1.19 interrogative
1.20 declarative
1.21-1.25 Examples:
1.21 My favorite time of year is autumn.
1.22 I enjoy boating and fishing.
1.23 Charles has not missed Sunday school for five years.
1.24 Betty and I will bake cookies now.
1.25 Sam hit a home run to win the game for our team.
1.26-1.31 Examples:
1.26 Who sat next to you at church last night?
1.27 What did you eat for lunch today?
1.28 Which way shall we go?
1.29 When will your brother come home?
1.30 How can you be tired after your nap?
1.31 Where are you going on your vacation?
1.32 Have you finished your report?
1.33 Can cats climb trees?
1.34 Must I go to bed now?
1.35 May I have a slice of pie?
1.36 Can you return your library book?
1.37-1.41 Examples:
1.37 Shall we leave now?
1.38 Did you sleep well?
1.39 Will you be finished soon?
1.40 Was the book enjoyable?
1.41 Does your puppy chase the cat?

1.42-1.46 Examples:
1.42 Do not forget your lunch.
1.43 Please bring me that book.
1.44 Stop!
1.45 Will you close the door?
1.46 Hand me the hammer.
1.47-1.51 Examples:
1.47 Tommy's stuck in the tree!
1.48 You've ruined your new pants!
1.49 Those bees are coming back!
1.50 Here he is!
1.51 It can't be true!
1.52 declarative
1.53 interrogative
1.54 imperative
1.55 exclamatory
1.56 tangible
1.57 auxiliary verbs
1.58 exclamation mark
1.59 question mark
1.60 period
1.61 period
1.62 Jesus and His disciples were resting in the desert near the city of Bethsaida. When the people learned where Jesus was, they followed Him. Jesus received them. He told them of the kingdom of God.
Toward evening His disciples asked Jesus to send the people to get food.
Jesus answered, "Give ye them to eat."
The disciples had only five loaves and two fishes. "How can we feed five thousand people?" they asked.
Jesus took the five loaves and the two fishes. Looking up to heaven, He blessed them. Then he broke the bread and divided the fishes. Every person had all he could eat. After the meal, the disciples gathered up twelve baskets of food that remained.
1.63-1.70 Examples:
1.63 Next summer I may go to Montana.
1.64 I saw Tom on the football field after school.
1.65 That is the charcoaled roast that mother forgot about and left in the oven too long.
1.66 Did you ever get hiccups that just wouldn't quit?
1.67 If that phone rings one more time, I'll have to have it disconnected!

1.68 I have to get a signed permission slip before I can go on the field trip.

1.69 I'll call when the popcorn is ready.

1.70 I am trying to be fair because he is my friend, after all.

1.71-1.78 Examples:

1.71 The days are warmer. It will soon be summer.

1.72 Gerald cannot go hiking because his ankle is not healed.

1.73 Although cats are fine pets, I would rather have a dog.

1.74 I love to sing Christmas carols even though I cannot always carry the tune.

1.75 If you plant the seeds too deeply, they will not come up.

1.76 Have you finished your book report? I have not even started mine yet.

1.77 Sandy is bringing potato salad and Lee is bringing hot dogs. We will have a picnic in the park.

1.78 Tim earns extra money when he helps his neighbors do yard work on Saturdays.

1.79 The professor said that because thousands of high school graduates could not pass the college entrance exams they were rejected. Most of these deficiencies could have been prevented by a proper education. This fact proved that public education was bad and that something ought to be done about it.

1.80 Any order:
 a. question
 b. sequence
 c. request
 d. quiet
 e. frequent
 f. conquer

1.81 Any order:
 a. classification
 b. function
 c. question
 d. punctuation
 e. conversion
 f. provision
 g. opinion
 h. introduction
 i. exclamation
 j. pronunciation

1.82 Any order:
 a. classification
 b. vessel
 c. command
 d. pattern
 e. excellent

SELF TEST 1

1.01 f
1.02 h
1.03 l
1.04 e
1.05 g
1.06 m
1.07 k
1.08 d
1.09 b
1.010 a
1.011 Any order:
 a. fragments
 b. run-ons
 c. comma splices
1.012 to give a command
1.013 negative command
1.014 Any order:
 a. period
 b. exclamation mark
 c. question mark
1.015 decreases emphasis
1.016 a. ?
 b. interrogative
1.017 a. !
 b. imperative
1.018 a. !
 b. exclamation
1.019 a. .
 b. declarative
1.020 a. .
 b. imperative
1.021 a. .
 b. declarative
1.022 a. ?
 b. imperative
1.023 a. ?
 b. interrogative
1.024 a. .
 b. declarative
1.025 a. !
 b. imperative
1.026 complete
1.027 fragment
1.028 complete
1.029 fragment
1.030 run-on
1.031 fragment
1.032 comma splice
1.033 complete
1.034 run-on
1.035 fragment

1.036-1.040 Examples:
1.036 After we took down the tent, we packed the camper and left.
1.037 I just painted that chair, even though the paint does not look wet.
1.038 A strong wind came up. The boats broke loose from the dock, and they drifted away.
1.039 If you can hit a line drive, we want you on our team.
1.040 I hope you left the porch light on because we will not be home until late tonight.
or
I cannot see to study because it is too dark in here.
or
A penalty was called because the runner was out of bounds.

SECTION 2

2.1 paragraph
2.2 topic sentence
2.3 unity
2.4 sequence
2.5 indent
2.6 no
2.7 no
2.8 no
2.9 no
2.10 Today was a day when everything seemed to go wrong.
2.11 a. First I overslept.
  b. Because of that, I almost missed my bus.
  c. Then I realized I had forgotten my library book.
  d. In my last period gym class, I hurt my ankle.
  e. When the time came to go home I could not open my locker.
  f. Tomorrow I promise myself I will wake up on time!
  g. My hobby is stamp collecting.
2.12 –
2.13 + fact
2.14 + attitude or feeling
2.15 –
2.16 + definition
2.17 + opinion
2.18 + time and place
2.19 + definition
2.20 + question
2.21-2.26 Examples:
2.21 Definition —
Bowling is an indoor sport in which a heavy ball is rolled down a wooden lane toward ten wooden pins arranged in a triangular shape.
2.22 Fact —
You should use a ball that fits your hand and that is the correct weight.
2.23 Opinion —
I think a hard rubber ball is better than a plastic one.
2.24 Time and place —
Last summer my family bowled once a week.
2.25 Attitude or feeling —
I really was proud to score a 150 game!
2.26 Question —
Have you ever tried to bowl?
2.27 main or central idea
2.28 formal
2.29 implied or suggested

2.30 no

2.31 no

2.32 no

2.33 Each winter we feed the wild birds.

2.34 yes

2.35 yes

2.36 no

2.37 Any order:
a. feed
b. crumbs
c. seeds
d. suet
e. fruit
f. feeder tray
g. eat
h. feeder

2.38 Teacher check

2.39 Why was Paul known as the "Apostle to the Gentiles"?

2.40 yes

2.41 chronological sequence

2.42 yes

2.43 Teacher check

2.44 Teacher check

2.45 a. yes
b. yes

2.46 a. Wild animals do not always make good pets.
b. yes
c. yes

2.47 a. 14
b. yes

2.48 As Tubby grew bigger and stronger, our laughter stopped.

2.49 Examples:
a. when
b. at first
c. as
d. finally

2.50 Teacher check

2.51 Teacher check

2.52-2.65 Teacher check

2.66 nouns

2.67 adjectives

2.68 transitive

2.69 repetitive

2.70 definitive

2.71 promotive

2.72 communicative

2.73 deduction

2.74 induction

2.75 creation

2.76 instruction

2.77 relation

2.78 legislation

2.79 nation

2.80 meditation

2.81 to indent

2.82 to sum

2.83 to compose

2.84 to confirm

2.85 to resolve

2.86 to save

SELF TEST 2

2.01	false
2.02	true
2.03	false
2.04	true
2.05	true
2.06	true
2.07	true
2.08	true
2.09	false
2.10	true
2.011	d
2.012	k
2.013	m
2.014	n
2.015	i
2.016	a
2.017	l
2.018	c
2.019	r
2.020	b
3.021	e
2.022	h
2.023	g
2.024	j
2.025	q
2.026	f

2.027 deductive paragraph –
The paragraph starts with the topic sentence.
The rest of the sentences explain or support it.

2.028 inductive paragraph –
The paragraph consists of various sentences
building up to the topic sentence that ends
the paragraph.

2.029 auxiliary verb –
A verb that helps express a meaning that one
verb alone could not.

2.030 comma-splice error –
A sentence error created by joining two
complete sentences with only a comma.

2.031 transition –
Some element that links or connects
something following with something
preceding it.

2.032 run-on sentence –
Two or more main clauses run together by
excessive use of <u>and</u> and <u>so</u>.

2.033 chronological order –
Events arranged in sequence; in the order in
which they occurred: first, second, third...

2.034	paragraph
2.035	indention
2.036	unity
2.037	sequence
2.038	transitional
2.039	implied or suggested
2.040	conclusion, summary, or climax
2.041	complexity
2.042	topic sentence

2.043 Any one answer:
novels
short stories
newspaper articles
informal writing

SECTION 3

3.1	fär´mə sē
3.2	fōn
3.3	fō´tə grăf´
3.4	frāz
3.5	fĭz´ĭks
3.6	a. ī´lənd
	b. s
3.7	a. dĕt
	b. b
3.8	a. nīf
	b. k, e
3.9	a. săm´ən
	b. l
3.10	a. gōst
	b. h
3.11	a. līt
	b. gh
3.12	kûr´nəl
3.13	chôk
3.14	shär´lə-tən
3.15	kăz´əm
3.16	chăs´ē (-ēz), shăs´ē
3.17	shō´fər, shō-fûr´
3.18	chĕk
3.19	krĭs´chən
3.20	a. ĕs´kôrt´
	b. ĭ-skôrt´, ĕ-skôrt´, ĕs´kôrt´
3.21	a. prŏd´o͞os, prō´do͞os
	b. prə-do͞os´, -dyo͞os´, prō-
3.22	a. lĕd
	b. lēd
3.23	a. rĕb´əl
	b. rĭ-bĕl´
3.24	a. rĕk´ərd
	b. rĭ-kôrd´
3.25	a. rē´fŭnd´
	b. rĭ-fŭnd´
3.26	a. wĭnd
	b. wīnd
3.27	a. kŏm´bīn´
	b. kəm-bīn´
3.28	a. rēd
	b. rĕd
3.29	a. wo͞ond
	b. wound

3.30-3.34 Examples:

3.30 refund —
    a. Did you get a refund?
    (noun)
    b. The store will refund your money.
    (verb)

3.31 combine —
    a A combine is used to harvest wheat.
    (noun)
    b. Combine milk and cream in that pitcher.
    (verb)

3.32 read —
    a. Have you read *Treasure Island*?
    (past tense)
    b. I plan to read it next.
    (infinitive)

3.33 wound —
    a. The doctor dressed his wound.
    (noun)
    b. He wound the string around his finger.
    (verb)

3.34 record —
    a. The record is broken.
    (noun)
    b. Did you record those scores?
    (verb)

3.35-3.44 Pronunciations circled will vary according to regions.

3.35	pĭ-kän´, -kăn´, pē´kăn
3.36	ro͞ot, rout
3.37	do͞o, dyo͞o
3.38	lĕv´ər, lē´vər
3.39	tə mā´tō, tə mä´tō
3.40	ē´*thər*, ī´*thər*)
3.41	ko͞o´pŏn, kyo͞o´-
3.42	jo͞o´və nīl´, -nəl
3.43	ănt, änt
3.44	lăb´rə tôr´ē
3.45	Teacher check
3.46	Teacher check
3.47	a. library
	b. lī´brĕr´ē
3.48	a. history
	b. hĭs´tə rē
3.49	a. laboratory
	b. lăb´rə tôr´ē
3.50	a. escape
	b. ĭ skāp´
3.51	a. surprise
	b. sər prīz´
3.52	a. wash
	b. wŏsh, wôsh

3.53 a. sophomore
b. sŏf´ə môr, sŏf´môr
3.54 a. geography
b. jē ŏg´rə fē
3.55 a. mathematics
b. măth´ə măt´ĭks
3.56 a. literature
b. lĭt´ər ə chŏŏr, -chər
3.57 Teacher check
3.58 Example:
There was an Old Man in a tree,
who was horribly bored by a Bee;
   When they said, "Does it buzz?"
   He replied, "Yes, it does!"
"It's a regular brute of a Bee!"
3.59 OPTIONAL ACTIVITY: Teacher check
3.60 a. chôr´tl
b. snorting, joyful laugh, or chuckle
a. gə lŭmf
b. move, run, or gallop clumsily or heavily
a. pĕk
b. unit of dry volume or capacity (1/4 bushel)
a. pound
b. weight equal to 16 ounces (453.592 grams)
a. rŭn´sə bəl spōōn
b. fork-like spoon that has a cutting edge
a. shĭl´ĭng
b. UK coin worth one twentieth of a pound
a. stīl
b. set or series of steps crossing a fence or wall
a. vĕl´əm
b. parchment used for pages and binding books
3.61 c
3.62 b
3.63 c
3.64 d
3.65 b
3.66 a
3.67 a
3.68 c
3.69 ə gĕn´
3.70 ăth lĕt´ĭks
3.71 ə tăkt´
3.72 bör´o, bôr´o
3.73 chĭl´drən
3.74 kōō´pŏn, kyōō´pŏn
3.75 dround
3.76 ĭ-skāp´
3.77 fĕb´rōō ĕr ē, fĕb´yōō-
3.78 gŭv´ərn mənt
3.79 verb: grăj´ōō āt; noun: grăj´ōō ĭt

3.80 hăv ĭng
3.81 hīt
3.82 ī´ərn
3.83 lī´brĕr´ē
3.84 ô´fən, ŏf´ən, ôf´tən, ŏf´tən
3.85 rĭns
3.86 stŭm´ək
3.87 sər prīz´
3.88 sə spĭsh´ən
3.89 tīrd
3.90 wŏsh, wôsh
3.91 rench
3.92 yĕs´tər dā, -dē
3.93-3.97 Examples:
3.93 <u>Athletics</u> is <u>often</u> considered bad for the <u>stomach</u>.
3.94 An <u>iron</u> <u>wrench</u> <u>escaped</u> <u>again</u> <u>yesterday</u> from a <u>tired</u> father's tool chest, but three <u>surprised</u> <u>children</u> are under <u>suspicion</u>.
3.95 In <u>February</u> I <u>borrowed</u> a plate which I must <u>wash</u> and <u>rinse</u> before returning.
3.96 In the <u>library</u> he read a <u>government</u> report saying that a <u>graduate</u> had <u>attacked</u> a <u>coupon</u>.
3.97 The <u>height</u> of <u>suspicion</u> surrounds a <u>drowned</u> book which may have been <u>borrowed</u>.

SELF TEST 3

3.01 l
3.02 e
3.03 m
3.04 c
3.05 i
3.06 f
3.07 a
3.08 d
3.09 g
3.010 h
3.011 false
3.012 false
3.013 true
3.014 false
3.015 false
3.016 true
3.017 true
3.018 true
3.019 true
3.020 true
3.021 pseudonym
3.022 rhyme
3.023 tongue twister
3.024 nonsense
3.025 alliterative
3.026 coined
3.027 limerick
3.028 rhythm
3.029 unity
3.030 sequence
3.031 the work or action normally performed;
         purpose
3.032 something that can be seen or touched
3.033 reasoning from general to particular
3.034 final presentation of facts
3.035 link between ideas or events;
         a paragraph preceding paragraph with one
         following
3.036 b
3.037 d
3.038 a
3.039 d
3.040 b

LIFEPAC TEST

1. j
2. c
3. k
4. i
5. b
6. e
7. l
8. h
9. a
10. o
11. false
12. true
13. false
14. true
15. true
16. true
17. false
18. false
19. true
20. false
21. c
22. a
23. d
24. a
25. c
26. a
27. b
28. c
29. b
30. c
31. Lewis Carroll
32. Any order:
    a. period
    b. exclamation mark
    c. question mark
33. deductive
34. limerick
35. alliterative
36. rhyme
37. rhythm
38. anonymous
39. Any order:
    a. fragments
    b. run-ons
    c. comma splices

ALTERNATE LIFEPAC TEST

1. f
2. d
3. i
4. g
5. a
6. h
7. k
8. j
9. b
10. e
11. interrogative
12. declarative
13. sentence
14. fragment
15. Either order:
    a. limericks
    b. tongue-twisters
16. communicates a complete thought
17. comma splice
18. run-ons
19. deductive
20. articulation
21. coined
22. a
23. d
24. d
25. false
26. false
27. false
28. true
29. true
30. false

SPELLING TEST

1	abstract	Kandinsky was an **abstract** painter.	abstract
2	auxiliary	Hospitals use **auxiliary** power units in case of emergencies.	auxiliary
3	believe	I **believe** Susan went in the wrong direction.	believe
4	classification	Each **classification** of cacti was represented in the garden.	classification
5	command	He had the power to **command** respect.	command
6	conquer	By trusting God we can **conquer** our worst fears.	conquer
7	continue	Let's **continue** our discussion of the apostles.	continue
8	conversion	The **conversion** of heat and mechanical energy produce electrical energy.	conversion
9	describe	I can't **describe** how happy I feel.	describe
10	excellent	Paul played an **excellent** game of chess.	excellent
11	exclamation	Her **exclamation** came as a surprise.	exclamation
12	frequent	The senators would **frequent** the White House.	frequent
13	function	Our telephone could not **function** without being serviced.	function
14	introduction	A short **introduction** preceded the novel.	introduction
15	lightning	In the middle of the storm, **lightning** struck one of our trees.	lightning
16	opinion	I'd like to hear your **opinion** of the event.	opinion
17	pattern	Sometimes we **pattern** our speech like our friends.	pattern
18	pronunciation	Is that the correct **pronunciation** of the word?	pronunciation
19	persecute	Lawyers should not **persecute** their opponent's clients.	persecute
20	provision	There was no **provision** made for the extra people coming.	provision
21	punctuation	Did you proof the letter for correct **punctuation**?	punctuation
22	question	If you have a **question**, please raise your hand.	question
23	quiet	Please remain **quiet** while you are in the library.	quiet
24	request	I have just one **request** to make of you.	request
25	rhythm	The **rhythm** of the horse's movement could be seen.	rhythm

SPELLING TEST

26	communication	It is important for you and me to have proper **communication**.	communication
27	confirmation	She gave me her **confirmation** over the phone.	confirmation
28	composition	Have you all written your **composition** on friendship?	composition
29	creation	By the seventh day, God's **creation** of the world was complete.	creation
30	creative	Debbie wrote a remarkably **creative** poem.	creative
31	cumulative	The blustering wind had a **cumulative** effect during the day.	cumulative
32	deductive	That was **deductive** reasoning on your part.	deductive
33	definition	The red brick fence gave **definition** to our property.	definition
34	devotion	Early each morning was our time of **devotion** to the Lord.	devotion
35	indention	When writing a paragraph, use a five-space **indention**.	indention
36	inductive	The **inductive** committee met to decide the issue.	inductive
37	instructive	Our Sunday Bible study was spiritual as well as **instructive**.	instructive
38	legislative	In Washington, D.C., the **legislative** committees have tremendous power.	legislative
39	meditative	Margie's quietness made her seem **meditative**.	meditative
40	native	The Saguaro cactus is **native** to Arizona.	native

LANGUAGE ARTS 709

ALTERNATE LIFEPAC TEST

NAME _____

DATE _____

SCORE _____

54
___
68

Match these items (each answer, 2 points).

1. _____ climax		a. a short, lively story
2. _____ unity		b. a mark used to indicate pronunciation
3. _____ transition		c. author's name unknown
4. _____ deductive		d. having one main idea
5. _____ anecdote		e. words beginning with the same sound (letter)
6. _____ function		f. the high point
7. _____ phonetic		g. from the general to the particular
8. _____ sequence		h. use
9. _____ diacritical		i. element linking one part to another
10. _____ alliterative		j. logical order
		k. having to do with speech sounds

Complete these sentences (each answer, 3 points).

11. A sentence that asks a question is called _____ .

12. The most common type of English sentence is _____ .

13. The basic structure of communication is the _____ .

14. An incomplete sentence is a(n) _____ .

15. Two types of nonsense verse are a. _____ and b. _____ .

16. A sentence is a group of words that _____

    _____ .

17. Two complete sentences incorrectly joined by a comma make a(n) _____

    _____ .

18. Sentences having excessive coordination are called _____ .

19. A paragraph in which the topic sentence comes first is an example of the

    _____ pattern.

20. The clear, distinct pronunciation of speech sounds is called _____ .

21. Many nonsense words have been made up or _____ .

Write the letter for the correct answer on each line (each answer, 2 points).

22. The correctly spelled word is _____ .
    a. repetition   b. comulutive   c. medetative   d. atheletics

23. The correctly spelled word is _____ .
    a. beleive   b. auxilliary   c. lightening   d. tangible

24. Which statement about sentences is *not* true? _____
    a. Sentences are punctuated as independent units.
    b. Sentence fragments are commonly used in casual conversation.
    c. Four types of sentences are possible.
    d. To make an idea in a sentence more important, subordinate it.

Answer *true* **or** *false* (each answer, 1 point).

25. _____ An imperative question asks a question.

26. _____ Verse with foolish words having no serious meaning is called *runcible*.

27. _____ You can be assured that a paragraph has unity if it has a topic sentence.

28. _____ Correct pronunciation is vital to effective communication.

29. _____ A good example of nonsense verse is "Jabberwocky" by Lewis Carroll.

30. _____ An anonymous poem is one whose author uses another name.

ALTERNATE SPELLING TEST

1	preposition	A **preposition** is one of the eight parts of speech.	preposition
2	promotion	My sister received a **promotion** for her excellent work.	promotion
3	relative	Linda brought up a subject which was not **relative** to our discussion.	relative
4	resolution	Can you stay with your **resolution**?	resolution
5	repetition	Hearing the **repetition** of the Bible verse helped me to remember it.	repetition
6	salvation	**Salvation** is a gift from God.	salvation
7	summation	Write down the **summation** of your thoughts on the effects of air pollution.	summation
8	tradition	Going to sunrise service became a **tradition** with our family.	tradition
9	transition	I went through a **transition** period last year when we moved.	transition
10	again	Jennifer's friends asked her to sing the hymn **again**.	again
11	athletics	Our school has a fine **athletics** program.	athletics
12	attacked	Paul **attacked** the ball with tremendous vigor.	attacked
13	borrow	Ann asked to **borrow** my bike for the day.	borrow
14	children	It was heartwarming to see all our **children** happy.	children
15	coupon	Each Boy Scout had one **coupon** left to sell.	coupon
16	drowned	My small puppy almost **drowned** in the lake.	drowned
17	escape	I could not **escape** feeling sad that summer vacation was over.	escape
18	February	George Washington's birthday is **February**, 22.	February
19	government	Do you take an interest in your local **government**?	government
20	graduate	I'm looking forward to the day I **graduate**.	graduate
21	having	Pat was **having** a very productive day.	having
22	height	When Richard stood up, his **height** was tremendous.	height
23	iron	Early American women used large **iron** kettles to cook in.	iron
24	library	It is exciting to read all the new books in our **library**.	library

ALTERNATE SPELLING TEST

25	often	How **often** do you read your Bible?	often
26	rinse	Mom asked me to **rinse** my clothes thoroughly.	rinse
27	surprise	We gave a **surprise** birthday party for my teacher.	surprise
28	suspicion	I had a **suspicion** he was corning.	suspicion
29	stomach	Doing sit-ups each day will help strengthen your **stomach** muscles.	stomach
30	tired	Riding my bike 20 miles made me very **tired**.	tired
31	wash	Stephen, would you help Dad **wash** the car?	wash
32	wrench	The mechanic misplaced his **wrench**.	wrench
33	yesterday	**Yesterday**, we had a day off from school.	yesterday
34	abstract	Kandinsky was an **abstract** painter.	abstract
35	auxiliary	Hospitals use **auxiliary** power units in case of emergencies.	auxiliary
36	believe	I **believe** Susan went in the wrong direction.	believe
37	classification	Each **classification** of cacti was represented in the garden.	classification
38	command	He had the power to **command** respect.	command
39	conquer	By trusting God we can **conquer** our worst fears.	conquer
40	continue	Let's **continue** our discussion of the apostles.	continue

LANGUAGE ARTS 710

Unit 10: Looking Back

TEACHER NOTES

MATERIALS NEEDED FOR LIFEPAC	
Required	Suggested
None	• since this is a review LIFEPAC, the students should have access to the entire Language Arts 700 series for clarification of information and additional practice • magazines, newspapers, or nonfiction books • reference books or online sources

ADDITIONAL LEARNING ACTIVITIES

Section 1: The Structure of Language

1. Have students write several sentences on the board and pick out the parts of speech studied in this series.

2. Have students identify the pattern of sentences you have written on the board or on duplicated sheets.

3. Have a "language bee." Let one person ask a definition or a question about language structure. Members of the group who miss must go to the back of the line. Have a champion "play off" between the top players in various groups.

4. Make a poster with rules for using various parts of speech you have studied.

5. Make a cartoon showing errors in sentences or misunderstanding because of sentence or word errors.

Section 2: The Mechanics of Language

1. Write a paragraph on the board or make copies for the students to capitalize and punctuate.

2. Choose a punctuation mark that presents a special problem for you. Find examples of its use. Which rule fits the usage?

Section 3: The Skills of Communication

1. Choose some activity or story that would have chronological sequence. Scramble the events or steps and write them on the board or on a duplicated sheet. Have the students arrange these items in chronological sequence. (Examples: "How to Construct a Kite," "How to Set a Table," "How to Make Ice Cream," "How to Bathe a Dog," and so forth.)

2. Prepare a presentation of one or more types of listening. Set up some activity which requires that type of listening and present it to another group or the whole class.

3. Write a well-constructed paragraph with a topic sentence. Check your paragraph for unity, sequence, coordination and subordination, as well as for capitalization and punctuation. Turn in the revised copy.

Administer the LIFEPAC Spelling Test.

The test is provided in this Teacher's Guide.

Evaluate the tests and review the words the students spelled incorrectly.

If necessary, review all of the words in the unit to prepare for the alternate spelling test.

Administer the Alternate LIFEPAC Spelling test that is provided in this Teacher's Guide.

Administer the LIFEPAC Test.

The test is to be administered in one session. Give no help except with directions.

Evaluate the tests and review areas where the students have done poorly.

Review the pages and activities that stress the concepts tested.

If necessary, administer the Alternate LIFEPAC Test.

ANSWER KEYS

SECTION 1

1.1 a. laughed
b. shall laugh
1.2 a. requested
b. shall request
1.3 a. played
b. will play
1.4 a. sailed
b. will sail
1.5 a. sewed
b. will sew
1.6 Examples:
a. The team plays ball on Thursdays.
b. Mom bakes bread every Friday.
c. Mr. Burns is raking his front yard.
d. I see you behind the car.
e. The children are playing in the yard.
1.7 Examples:
a. Mom baked bread yesterday.
b. Mr. Buckley drove his car to work.
c. The teacher taught the class to spell.
d. Jonathan wrote a letter to Jack.
e. I told him to sit down.
1.8 Examples:
a. I shall play with you after school.
b. Jack will learn to play the piano.
c. I shall ask Bill to help me with my homework.
d. Will you visit me next week?
e. Mr. Borrows will mow his lawn on Saturday.
1.9 a. have asked
b. had asked
c. will have asked
1.10 a. have swum
b. had swum
c. will have swum
1.11 a. have built
b. had built
c. will have built
1.12 a. have driven
b. had driven
c. will have driven
1.13 a. have spoken
b. had spoken
c. will have spoken

1.14 Examples:
a. I have asked you to help me many times.
b. Mr. Adams has written a book about cats.
c. We have walked five miles already.
d. He has sent a letter to his Congressman.
e. Mrs. Jones has baked ten pies for the party.
1.15 Examples:
a. We had run after our lost dog.
b. My brother had broken Mom's favorite vase.
c. Mr. James had spoken before we interrupted.
d. The children had hoped they'd win the contest.
e. My friends had planned a trip to the ocean.
1.16 Examples:
a. We shall have finished by then.
b. Mary will have baked five pies by the time she finishes.
c. Jack will have raised ten dogs if he keeps up at this rate.
d. He will have drawn many portraits before he retires.
e. Dawn will have spoken before our club four times after the next meeting.

1.17-1.26

	Subject	Verb
1.17	God	loves
1.18	President	speaks
1.19	family, I,	attend
1.20	You	receive
1.21	One	writes
1.22	mother, father,	read
1.23	Margarine	substitutes
1.24	Jack	catches
1.25	pile	burns
1.26	I	worship
1.27	rising	
1.28	raised	
1.29	sit	
1.30	lay	
1.31	sat	
1.32	setting	
1.33	laying	
1.34	raising	
1.35	lie	
1.36	rose	

1.37   a. snake
           b. lettuce
1.38   Naomi, Moab, daughters-in-law, companion,
           Ruth, journey, mother-in-law
1.39-1.48

Pronoun	Antecedent
1.39 she	Sarah
1.40 it	truck
1.41 they	members
1.42 his	boy
1.43 we	you, I
1.44 it	model
1.45 it	book
1.46 I	bride
1.47 his	John
1.48 it	car

1.49   a. nominative
           b. She is my sister.
1.50   a. objective
           b. Jack saw her at the game.
1.51   a. possessive
           b. My mother made my new dress.
1.52   he
1.53   he
1.54   me
1.55   we
1.56   hers
1.57   he
1.58   she
1.59   us
1.60   your
1.61   his
1.62   Examples:
           a. I hurt myself.
           b. Jack locked himself outside.
           c. Jennifer gave herself a facial.
           d. The dog scratched itself.
           e. We shall draw ourselves in art class.
           f. The children dressed themselves quickly.
           g. Don't take yourself too seriously.
           h. Help yourselves to the chips and
               lemonade.
1.63   Either order:
           a. that
           b. those
1.64   Either order:
           a. this
           b. these
1.65   Either order:
           a. this
           b. that
1.66   Either order:
           a. these
           b. those

1.67   Teacher check
1.68   Jesus died for man's sins. He was crucified.
1.69   Karen gave her mother some candy. It was
           delicious.
1.70   George broke his leg yesterday.
1.71   Donna and Barbara completed their science
           projects early.

1.72   their
1.73   their
1.74   he
1.75   She

1.76 tall	what kind
1.77 six	how many
1.78 good	what kind
1.79 patient	what kind
1.80 Seven	how many
1.81 new	what kind
1.82 young	which one *or* what kind
affectionate	what kind

1.83   The milk tasted sour.
1.84   Coin collecting is an interesting hobby.
1.85   Mount Whitney is the loftiest mountain in
           the United States.
1.86   The children had a pleasant time at the
           school picnic.
1.87   The weather became warm and
           uncomfortable.
1.88   I am glad that her difficulties are minor.
1.89   The friendly teacher greeted the new
           students.
1.90   We took the final exam on Saturday.
1.91   Mother was angry when I returned home
           late.
1.92   The Chinese people greeted their leader
           warmly.
1.93   The child looked hungrily at the food.
1.94   Tomorrow we shall go to the store.
1.95   The lion tamer glanced nervously at the
           animals in the cage.
1.96   Please bring the book here to me.
1.97   Try driving carefully.
1.98   Her hair is quite long.
1.99   Judith very nearly won the spelling contest.

1.100 Examples:
 a. Jackie lives over *there*.
 b. Sit *here* next to me.

1.101 Examples:
 a. *Yesterday* I sold my car.
 b. Jackie stayed after school *today*.

1.102 Examples:
 a. The horses raced *swiftly* to the finish line.
 b. The children played *happily* in the sun.

1.103 Examples:
 a. She drank *too* much juice.
 b. The baby is not *very* big.

1.104 Examples:
 a. Mark ran *very* fast in the race.
 b. Kenny can jump *quite* high.

1.105 Jack and Jill ran up the hill.
 adverb

1.106 The floor of the bedroom is dusty.
 adjective

1.107 I don't like shirts with short sleeves.
 adjective

1.108 With wide eyes he started at us.
 adverb

1.109 We saw the tornado moving across the sky.
 adverb

1.110 Mr. Thompson discovered the lost papers in the drawer.
 adverb

1.111 My dad gave my brother a bike on his tenth birthday.
 adverb

1.112 Above the door of my bedroom hung a horseshoe.
 adverb; adjective

1.113 Examples:
 a. The door of the old house is broken.
 b. The girl with the long hair is my sister.

1.114 Examples:
 a. After the party we went out to eat.
 b. Jack climbed the hill before Jill.

1.115 Examples:
 a. We ate dinner at the restaurant.
 b. Today we will watch the game from the stands.

1.116 a 1
 b. 2
 c. 5
 d. 3
 e. 2
 f. 3
 g. 5
 h. 4
 i. 4
 j. 1

1.117   s   v   I.O.   D.O.
 My father gave me a new football.

1.118   s   v   P.N.
 The present was a dollhouse.

1.119   s   v   P.A.
 The show was excellent.

1.120   s   v   I.O.   D.O.
 My dog brought Dad his bone.

1.121 Teacher check

1.122 a. declarative
 b. interrogative
 c. exclamatory
 d. declarative
 e. imperative
 f. interrogative
 g. declarative
 h. interrogative
 i. exclamatory
 j. imperative

1.123 Examples:
 a. I saw Mr. James yesterday.
 b. Birds fly in the sky.
 c. Are you going to the game?
 d. Did Mom bake those pies for the party?
 e. Get the book for me.
 f. Sit in that chair.
 g. Quick! The house is on fire!
 h. Help! I'm drowning!

1.124 Teacher check

1.125 Teacher check

1.126 Any order:
 a. achieve
 b. relief
 c. impatience

1.127 Any order:
 a. foreigner
 b. receive
 c. neighbor
 d. their

1.128 Any order:
   a. possessive
   b. grammar
   c. recommend
   d. uninterrupted
   e. embarrassed
   f. communicate
   g. agreeable

1.129 Any order:
   a. there
   b. their
   c. they're
   d. threw
   e. through
   f. to
   g. two
   h. too

1.130 <u>Across</u>
   2. humorous
   3. argument
   4. judgment
   6. compel
   8. courteous
   13. label
   14. angel
   15. finally
   19. famous
   20. individual
   21. correctly
   23. previous
   24. government

<u>Down</u>
   1. mysterious
   3. angle
   5. technical
   7. muscle
   9. temple
   10. original
   11. really
   12. woolly
   16. nickel
   17. logical
   18. parable
   22. temperament

1.131 Teacher check

SELF TEST 1

1.01 a verb
1.02 an adjective
1.03 adverb
1.04 tense
1.05 a sentence
1.06 Any order:
   a. preposition
   b. noun
   c. pronoun
1.07 pronoun
1.08 interrogative
1.09 declarative
1.010 exclamatory
1.011 imperative
1.012 a. ?
   b. interrogative
1.013 a. !
   b. exclamatory
1.014 a. .
   b. declarative
1.015 a. .
   b. declarative
1.016 a. ?
   b. interrogative
1.017 a. .
   b. imperative
1.018 Any order:
   a. present
   b. past
   c. future
   d. present perfect
   e. past perfect
   f. future perfect
1.019 Any order:
   a. subject – verb
   b. subject – verb – direct object
   c. subject – linking verb – predicate nominative
   d. subject – linking verb – predicate adjective
   e. subject – verb – indirect object – direct object
1.020 Any order:
   a. nominative
   b. objective
   c. possessive
1.021 Any order:
   a. this
   b. that
   c. those
   d. these

1.022 go
1.023 arrived
1.024 worked
1.025 will visit
1.026 her
1.027 its
1.028 yours
1.029 itself
1.030 him (her)
1.031 I (he, she)
1.032 their
1.033 Those (These)
1.034 hers
1.035 them
1.036 she
1.037 The solution in the test tube turned an odd color.
1.038 The happy children splashed merrily in the pool.
1.039 We are very happy.
1.040 The distinguished man in the suit is handsome.
1.041 Jack successfully produced three plays in August.
1.042
    s   v   D.O.   v
The cat grabbed the yarn and scampered away.
1.043
    s   v   P.A.
The dinner at the restaurant was delicious.
1.044
    s   v   I.O.   D.O.
Mother gave my little sister a doll for her birthday.
1.045
            s   v   P.N.
The first President was George Washington.
1.046
            s   v   I.O.   D.O.
The policeman gave the speeder a ticket.

SECTION 2

2.1 We, Our, Don, Sue, I, Boulder, Colorado, They, W. Colter Avenue, Rocky Lake, We, All, Saints Christian Church, Mr., Mrs. Charles'

2.2
a. Jack asked sue, "please help me with my assignment."
b. last winter we went to florida and visited miami, orlando, and many other Cities.
c. "Star light, star bright, first star i see tonight,
d. Wish I may, wish I might, have this wish come true tonight."
e. The students drank coke and rode in their parents' fords and chevrolets to mcDonalds.
f. My Family attends good shepherd Lutheran church.

2.3 Example:
"I like to play tennis," said Jane.

2.4 Example:
I saw Dr. Johns, Mr. Edwards, and Mrs. Dooley at the party.

2.5 Example:
Crest, Colgate, Ultra Bright, and Biotène all contain fluoride.

2.6 Example:
357 Eastham, Springfield, Ohio, United States

2.7 Examples:
a. France
b. Mississippi
c. Indian
d. Encanto Park

2.8 Example:
This year Christmas Day falls on a Tuesday in December.

2.9 Examples:
a. Mayflower Compact
b. Renaissance
c. Bicentennial of the United States

2.10 Example:
Aunt Ellen is here.

2.11 Example:
Little Women

2.12 Example:
God watches over all His children.

2.13   C
2.14   I
2.15   C
2.16   I
2.17   I
2.18 a. I
    b. C
2.19   I

2.20	possessive		**2.42**	<u>c</u>
2.21	contraction		**2.43**	<u>i</u>
2.22	's		**2.44**	<u>i</u>
2.23	'		**2.45**	<u>i</u>
2.24	an omitted letter		**2.46**	<u>i</u>
2.25	plural		**2.47**	<u>c</u>

2.26 Frank's

2.27 principal's

2.28 Sampson's

2.29 Cows'

2.30 dollars'

2.31 Nobody's

2.32 children's

2.33 babies'

2.34 theirs

2.35 week's

2.36 Examples:
a. I can't attend the banquet tomorrow night.
b. We shouldn't disturb the bird's nest.

2.37 Example:
Somebody's car was recently washed.

2.38 Example:
My dog's collar is broken.

2.39 Examples:
a. The boys' teams are ready to play.
b. Some women's clubs meet on Thursdays.

2.40 Example:
Mississippi has four s's in its spelling.

2.41
a. When he finished, the carpenter asked, "How do you like it?"
b. The poet read some lines from his poem, "The Lighthouse."
c. "Wait until I finish my chores," he said, "then I'll go with you."
d. The assignment for tonight in English is to read chapter 12, entitled, "The Great Depression."
e. "Did you get an A on your term paper?" Mary asked. "You worked so hard."
f. "The Interlopers," a short story by H.H. Munro, was discussed in my literature class.
g. I will finish my homework early so that I can listen to "The Gospel Hour."
h. The bus driver said, "To the west is the library. Buses stop there every quarter hour."
i. Have you read "A Narrow Escape" in this month's *Reader's Digest?*

2.48
a. 2.43
"Where are you going to school?" my new friend asked.
b. 2.44
She yelled, "Watch out for the car!"
c. 2.45
"I'm going to buy a new car," he said.
d. 2.46
"I'm going to call Janie," Sue said, "to ask her for the literature assignment."

2.49 Example:
Sue answered, "Yes, I'd love to go with you."

2.50 Example:
Sue said that she would like to go.

2.51 "Hi," Jane said to Julie, "I haven't seen you in a while."
"That's true," replied Julie. "I've been visiting my grandmother."
"Well, I'm glad you're back now."

2.52
a. parenthetic
b. supplementary
c. explanatory

2.53 numerical figures (numbers)

2.54 parentheses

2.55 Example:
Find the word in the dictionary.

2.56
a. twenty-three
b. fifty-five
c. ninety-eight

2.57 Example:
I think it is un-American to protest against the United States.

2.58 Example:
Ex-President Nixon visited the White House.

2.59
a. Yes, I saw the comedy show on television last night.
b. I have asked you three times already, Bill, to take out the trash.
c. Running all the way home, Dick tried to make it before the rain started falling.
d. Why, what a nice surprise!
e. After Diane finished the test, she sat back and relaxed.
f. Choking, Jeremy gasped for breath.
g. Tired and hungry, they returned from the twenty-mile hike.

2.60 false
2.61 true
2.62 false
2.63 true
2.64 true
2.65 false
2.66 a. Most short introductory phrases do not require commas.
b. An independent clause and a phrase do not have a comma between them.
c. A phrase does not contain a subject and a predicate.
2.67 a. Anna bought paint, a roller, and two brushes.
b. George, my older brother, joined the Army.
c. Mr. Weaver, who just joined the company, is the new vice president.
d. If all goes well, the house will be completed by March.
e. Yes, Janie has been accepted for the new job.
f. I looked for my friends in the library, in the cafeteria, and in the study hall.
g. Leslie, her knees shaking, walked on stage to receive her diploma.
h. He stood up, his teeth chattering, to brush the snow off his clothes.
2.68 a. Aunt Hazel, I think we should leave for home now.
b. You will agree, I hope, with the judge's decision.
c. She said, "Yes, I'll be glad to help you."
d. __NC__
e. I hope, Betty and Don, that you will come back and see us again.
f. Carl, John, Harry, Mike, and Larry make up the relay team.
g. __NC__
h. I cleaned the house, and Jack washed the dog.
i. __NC__
j. It is, to be sure, unfortunate.
k. In my opinion, that orchestra sounded off-key.
2.69 a. __A__
b. __QM__
c. __C__
d. __A__
e. __P__
f. __QM__
g. __H__
h. __C__

2.70   My father, Don, and I were vacationing on Nantucket Island off the coast of Massachusetts. We had left from home, which is Concord, New Hampshire, and had arrived at the ferry boat, Nantucket Queen, the next day. We rented a boat and sailed into Greber's Bay. The voices of other sailors, the sound of the water beneath us, and the overhead sails flapping were pleasant. Suddenly the peaceful scene was interrupted by shouts from another boat that had turned and was heading right into us.
    "Watch out!" two men yelled excitedly. "We've lost control of our boat!"
    "Grab the tiller, John!" Father yelled to me. "Pull it toward you when I give the signal."
    "All right, Dad," I responded.
    Dad grabbed the sail and as he adjusted it he yelled at me, "Now, John, pull back!"
    I did what he said not a moment too soon. Whew! What a narrow escape! The other boat passed within twenty-two inches of ours.

2.71 a. sentence
b. verb
c. predicate
d. noun
e. punctuation
f. preposition
g. fragment
h. adverb
i. subject
j. adjective
k. declarative
l. synonym
m. quotation
n. antonym

2.72 Word puzzle:

```
F  T  L  A  C  C  O  M  M  O  D  A  T  E  P  E
M  L  I  C  N  S  I  Q  S  M  O  C  T  N  N  V
T  M  M  S  N  N  H  S  Y  N  V  A  C  Y  O  I
S  O  P  A  P  P  Y  G  L  A  W  A  C  D  T  T
O  P  R  P  L  L  G  H  L  C  F  N  B  I  N  A
E  A  E  F  L  Q  Y  F  A  C  P  N  M  A  R  G
L  C  S  O  E  T  A  F  B  U  E  O  U  M  A  O
D  D  S  I  Y  B  I  D  L  R  Q  Y  T  F  C  R
D  E  I  O  Z  C  E  A  E  A  T  E  U  L  C  R
E  F  O  P  T  S  R  K  L  T  E  D  K  C  E  E
P  G  N  Q  S  D  J  P  U  E  R  G  O  O  N  T
F  O  O  E  A  J  E  T  V  S  M  T  M  U  T  N
O  Y  U  S  A  S  U  C  T  B  D  V  W  O  T  I
L  G  P  T  E  T  A  C  I  N  U  M  M  O  C  O
```

2.73 palr
2.74 four
2.75 reign
2.76 scent
2.77 rain
2.78 cent
2.79 pare
2.80 sent
2.81 for
2.82 rein
2.83 pear
2.84 fore
2.85 through
2.86 foul
2.87 road
2.88 sew
2.89 threw
2.90 sow
2.91 knew
2.92 write
2.93 flew
2.94 rode
2.95 right
2.96 so
2.97 blew
2.98 Teacher check

SELF TEST 2

2.01 true
2.02 true
2.03 false
2.04 false
2.05 true
2.06 false
2.07 true
2.08 _A_
2.09 _QM_
2.010 _P_
2.011 _A_
2.012 _QM_
2.013 _H_
2.014 _C_
2.015 _C_
2.016 _H_
2.017 jack and maryanne each drank a coca-cola as they walked Home from sunnyvale high school.
2.018 in the Summer we will travel to ocean city, new jersey.
2.019 the declaration of independence was signed july 4, 1776.
2.020 I read the grapes Of Wrath by john steinbeck.
2.021 Jack asked his Uncle to take him to see the lincoln memorial.
2.022 Dad's tools (including the wrenches) are in the toolbox.
2.023 Mother said, "Yes, you may go to Julie's party."
2.024 I might've accepted your invitation, if you'd asked sooner.
2.025 We all sang "My Country 'Tis of Thee" after the recitation of Lincoln's "Gettysburg Address."
2.026 "The cost of two (2) packages of envelopes and forty (40) rulers is twenty-five dollars ($25)," the supervisor said.
2.027 The boat sank on Monday, but why wasn't it found until today?
2.028 Our house is on fire!
2.029 Cautiously and hesitantly, Karen, hoping as we all did that she would be called upon, raised her hand to answer the question.
2.030 Our pastor, who is also the Boy Scout leader, said, "The next meeting of Troop 526 is cancelled."
2.031 Before Charles handed in his composition, he proofread the entire paper.

2.032 The camp counselor readily gave her swimming lessons.

2.033 We are looking for a man in a suit.

2.034 A crowd of spectators stood patiently waiting for the parade.

2.035 Three thousand people watched the colorful floats.

2.036 Today they will attend a fashion show of sport's clothes.

2.037-2.048 Examples:

2.037 I *lay* down to rest after school.

2.038 The sun will *rise* tomorrow at 6:00 a.m.

2.039 "*Set* that book on the table," said Jane to Bob.

2.040 Are you finished studying?

2.041 Come here, please.

2.042 I gave a gift to my friend.

2.043 I gave to Robert my prized possession.

2.044 Running beside the car, he called to the driver.

2.045 I wrote the play myself.

2.046 "Take this to your mother," Dad told me.

2.047 Her book is on the table.

2.048 A pretty girl happily played in the yard.

SECTION 3

3.1 Cannons nearly always betray an old wreck at the bottom of the ocean.

3.2 Last summer my family and I went camping in the Great Smokies.
At Christmas we went to Florida to see our grandparents.
A skunk is a small animal that has a bushy tail and a white stripe down its back.

3.3 There are many kinds of birds.
Example:
After much hard work it finally finishes.

3.4 It is an old bridge anyway.
Example:
Near the bridge is a path.

3.5 Jack nudged me.
Example:
The time passed so slowly.

3.6-3.10 Examples:

3.6 a. The players were soon covered with mud, *and* the spectators had difficulty identifying the teams.
b. The players were soon covered with mud, *so* the spectators had difficulty identifying the teams.

3.7 a. April is here, *but* the flowers are not in bloom.
b. April is here, *yet* the flowers are not in bloom.

3.8 a. I read the Bible, *so* I am a good Christian.
b. I read the Bible, *and* I am a good Christian.

3.9 a. The light turned red, *but* the car did not stop.
b. The light turned red, *yet* the car did not stop.

3.10 a. I will make a cake, *or* I might make a pie.
b. I will make a cake, *and* I might make a pie.

3.11-3.15 Examples:

3.11 Cats yawn *because* they have nothing else to do.

3.12 Bill arrived late for school *when* he overslept.

3.13 The cat crept forward slowly *until* the mouse ran into his hole.

3.14 Lucy was quiet *while* her little sister was sleeping.

3.15 You clean your room *after* you have a snack.

3.16 Teacher check

3.17 Teacher check

3.18 a. 9
     b. 1
     c. 4
     d. 7
     e. 2
     f. 10
     g. 3
     h. 5
     i. 8
     j. 6
3.19 b
3.20 c
3.21 a
3.22 a
3.23 Teacher check
3.24 Teacher check
3.25 a
3.26 c
3.27 f
3.28 h
3.29 i
3.30 critical
3.31 purposeful
3.32 passive
3.33 appreciative
3.34 critical
3.35 purposeful
3.36 purposeful
3.37 appreciative
3.38 Any order:
     –ance
     a. insurance
     b. acceptance
     c. allowance
3.39 Any order:
     –ence
     a. dependence
     b. residence
     c. patience
3.40 Any order:
     –ize
     a. civilize
     b. legalize
     c. minimize
3.41 Any order:
     –tion
     a. repetition
     b. imagination
     c. creation
     d. superstition

3.42 Any order:
     fore–
     a. foresight
     b. forecast
     c. forehead
3.43 Any order:
     –ment
     a. advancement
     b. advertisement
     c. excitement
     d. entertainment
3.44 Any order:
     double letters
     a. appropriate
     b. acceptance
     c. allowance
     d. appreciate
     e. opportunity
     f. borrow
     g. blessedness
3.45 Word puzzle:

3.46 a. effectively
     b. legislative
     c. spiritual
     d. urgent
     e. graciously
     f. factual
     g. often
     h. emotional
     i. yesterday
3.47 Nouns   Verbs
     a. authority   f. demonstrate
     b. cavity   g. meditate
     c. instructor   h. penetrated
     d. musician   i. portray
     e. stomach   j. summarize
3.48 Teacher check

SELF TEST 3

3.01	topic sentence		**3.029**	lie
3.02	sequence		**3.030**	set
3.03	coordinating conjunctions		**3.031**	rise
3.04	paragraph		**3.032**	tastes
3.05	apostrophe		**3.033**	done
3.06	stress		**3.034**	smells
3.07	pronoun		**3.035**	finished
3.08	verb		**3.036**	passive
3.09	critical listening		**3.037**	critical

3.10 chronological sequence

3.011 __7__

3.012 __5__ or __2__

3.013 __3__ or __5__

3.014 __1__

3.015 __6__ or __3__

3.016 I thought the vase was pretty.

3.017 __2__ or __4__

3.018 __4__ or __6__

3.019 The face of the clock on the pile read 3:00.
Note:
Other combinations of these sentences are possible. They should, however, flow in a logical sequence.

3.020 __11__

3.021 __8__

3.022 __10__

3.023 __9__

3.024 __12__

3.025 Examples:
a. My town needs many improvements to make it a better place to live.
b. You should practice good table manners when eating.
c. You are riding down a country road at night on your bicycle.

3.26 Hint:
The first sentence is usually the topic sentence. Use the five different sentence patterns you have learned in your paragraph.

3.27 a. Henry, James, and I played golf together.
b. The escaping convict dropped, a bullet in his leg.
c. Mrs. Stevenson, our cook, baked bread.

3.028 a. I live in Columbus, Ohio.
b. She said, "Never speak to me again!"
c. He is Peter's uncle.
d. He said, "I shall return."
e. I live at 654 W. Adam Street, Phoenix, Arizona.

or purposeful

3.038 appreciative

3.039 purposeful

3.040-3.049 Examples:

3.040 a. I wanted to go, but I had no money.
b. I wanted to go although I had no money.

3.041 a. He does not study, yet he gets good grades.
b. He does not study because he gets good grades.

3.042 a. He does not play the piano well, but he sings beautifully.
b. He does not play the piano well though he sings beautifully.

3.043 Will you pass me the butter, please?

3.044 That coat you're wearing is mine.

3.045 Get the dog inside.

3.046 His shoulder is hurt.

3.047 Danny walked four miles to school.

3.048 The pretty girl walked gracefully down the aisle.

3.049 While I was eating, I listened to the news report.

LIFEPAC TEST

1. true
2. false
3. false
4. false
5. true
6. true
7. true
8. false
9. true
10. false
11. coordinating conjunctions
12. adjectives
13. intonations
14. pronouns in the possessive case
15. demonstrative pronouns
16. a verb
17. parentheses
18. quotation mark
19. reflexive pronouns
20. Any order:
    a. present
    b. past
    c. future
    d. present perfect
    e. past perfect
    f. future perfect
21. Any order:
    a. declarative
    b. interrogative
    c. imperative
    d. exclamatory
22. Any order:
    a. nominative
    b. objective
    c. possessive
23. Any order:
    a. passive
    b. purposeful
    c. critical
    d. appreciative
24. Set
25. Lie
26. rise
27. drove, her
28. visit
29. her
30. mine
31. he
32. because
33. did

34. S-LV-P.N.
    The lovely children are my nephews.

35. S-V
    The large dog happily played with his bone.

36. S-V-D.O.
    Twenty students played musical instruments in the band.

37. S-LV-P.Adj.
    Some people are kind to others.

38. S-V-I.O.-D.O.
    The teacher readily gave the students a recess break.

39. He wrote a letter to my Mother.
40. jane and mary talked to dr. kelly.
41. I read the Book *charlotte's web* when i was in the third Grade.
42. We drank some pepsi at the westerville high school Football game.
43. My Birthday is february 22, the same day as george washington's.
44. Ralph replied, "I shall do as you say."
45. In college I took chemistry, Latin, history, and philosophy.
46. We can't forget Mom's birthday is September 27, 1990.
47. Your father-in-law, on the other hand, is a nice person.
48. I received your check for seventy dollars.
49. "Mind your p's and q's," said Mrs. Jenkins.
50. He came to our home, nevertheless, but did not stay long.

ALTERNATE LIFEPAC TEST

1. c

2. a

3. e

4. h

5. b

6. i

7. d

8. k

9. j

10. g

11. Any order:
a. declarative
b. interrogative
c. imperative
d. exclamatory

12. Any order:
a. nominative
b. objective
c. possessive

13. Any order:
a. present tense
b. past tense
c. past participle

14. Any order:
a. stress
b. pitch
c. juncture

15. Either order:
a. possession
b. contractions

16. When Naomi decided to leave Moab, her daughters-in-law went with her.

17. After the recitation of Lincoln's Gettysburg Address, we all sang "My Country 'Tis of Thee."

18. sit

19. rise

20. lay

21. false

22. true

23. true

24. false

25. true

26. false

27. true

28. false

29. false

30. false

31. Any order:
a. this
b. that
c. those
d. these

32. Any order:
a. passive
b. purposeful
c. critical
d. appreciative

33. c

34. e

35. a

36. b

37. b

38. b

39. b

40. d

SPELLING TEST

1	achieve	Trent was not able to **achieve** his goal.	achieve
2	communicate	Through sign language I was able to **communicate** with the deaf child.	communicate
3	foreigner	I am a **foreigner** when I visit their lands.	foreigner
4	neighbor	I asked my **neighbor** to go to church with me Sunday.	neighbor
5	principle	The science **principle** was difficult to understand.	principle
6	recommend	I **recommend** that several bridges be built over the river.	recommend
7	their	The children were eager to share **their** new found faith.	their
8	there	I put your shoes over **there** by the bookcase.	there
9	they're	Are you sure **they're** coming?	they're
10	to	Why don't we go **to** Hawaii this summer?	to
11	too	I liked to go skating, but my little brother always wanted to come, **too**.	too
12	two	We elect representatives every **two** years.	two
13	angel	The **angel** Gabriel was sent from God to Mary in Nazareth.	angel
14	angle	A right **angle** has ninety degrees.	angle
15	courteous	Mike, a **courteous** boy, held the door open for his sister.	courteous
16	government	It says in Romans that we should obey and pray for our **government**.	government
17	humorous	Mark's pantomime was quite **humorous**.	humorous
18	judgment	Christ will stand up for Christians at the final **judgment**.	judgment
19	logical	The Word of God is not only historical, it is also **logical**.	logical
20	nickel	You can hardly buy anything for a **nickel** anymore.	nickel
21	parable	Jesus told a **parable** about a sower.	parable
22	really	Do you **really** care about others?	really
23	technical	We do not have the **technical** knowledge to send a man to another solar system.	technical
24	temperament	Mary has a good-natured **temperament**.	temperament

SPELLING TEST

25	accommodate	The inn could not **accommodate** Joseph and Mary.	accommodate
26	adjective	An **adjective** is a descriptive word.	adjective
27	annoyed	Tom gets **annoyed** when the children are too noisy.	annoyed
28	threw	Mark **threw** the football down the field to his friend George.	threw
29	fragment	The policeman acquired only a **fragment** of information from the witness.	fragment
30	impression	Iris appeared to make a good **impression** on the new boss.	impression
31	noun	A **noun** is a person, place, or thing.	noun
32	predicate	The **predicate** expresses what is said about the subject.	predicate
33	punctuation	A good story needs proper **punctuation**.	punctuation
34	syllable	The word only had one **syllable**.	syllable
35	synonym	To keep from using the same word too often, you should find a **synonym** for that word.	synonym
36	cent	I spent every **cent** I had on a new Bible.	cent
37	for	I brought a piece of cherry pie just **for** you.	for
38	fore	There was a stained-glass window in the **fore** wall of the church.	fore
39	pair	I got a new **pair** of shoes for my birthday.	pair
40	pare	I had to **pare** twenty-two apples for the applesauce.	pare
41	pear	Alice found half a worm in her **pear**.	pear
42	scent	The air freshener had the **scent** of roses.	scent
43	sent	I **sent** a letter to my best friend in Ridley Park, Pennsylvania.	sent
44	write	When I grow up I would like to **write** a book.	write
45	acceptance	Mary Sue sought **acceptance** among her classmates.	acceptance
46	advancement	Jason's **advancement** through school was so rapid that he graduated from high school at the age of fifteen.	advancement
47	allowance	My parents give me a five dollar **allowance** each week.	allowance
48	blessedness	The **blessedness** of Christ's birth is recorded in the Bible.	blessedness

SPELLING TEST

49	civilize	Attempts were made to **civilize** the island's inhabitants.	civilize
50	dependence	A child's **dependence** on his parents is part of family structure.	dependence
51	excitement	There was much **excitement** on the eve of the President's visit.	excitement
52	forecast	The weather **forecast** was dismal.	forecast
53	foresight	She had the **foresight** to take along an extra pair of glasses.	foresight
54	insurance	I have a life **insurance** policy.	insurance
55	minimize	Lower speeds **minimize** the risks in driving.	minimize
56	patience	A fruit of the Spirit is **patience**.	patience
57	residence	My **residence** is in Groom, Texas.	residence
58	authority	God has given parents the **authority** to train and correct their children.	authority
59	demonstrate	The salesman wanted to **demonstrate** his vacuum cleaner.	demonstrate
60	emotional	Judy's response was **emotional** when her brother accepted Christ.	emotional
61	factual	Your report should be well researched and **factual**.	factual
62	instructor	My gymnastics **instructor** showed me how to walk on the beam.	instructor
63	iron	Each morning I **iron** my clothes for the day.	iron
64	meditate	We need to **meditate** on God's word daily.	meditate
65	often	I **often** find it difficult to get up in the morning.	often
66	portray	The painter tried to **portray** her as realistically as possible.	portray
67	request	Today Dad put in a **request** for vacation.	request
68	spiritual	Turning away from Jesus is a sign of **spiritual** decay.	spiritual
69	summarize	Our teacher wanted us to **summarize** the story we read.	summarize
70	wrench	One of the plumber's tools is a **wrench**.	wrench

LANGUAGE ARTS 710

ALTERNATE LIFEPAC TEST

NAME _____

DATE _____

SCORE _____

105
___
133

Match these items (each answer, 2 points).

1. _____ unity

2. _____ sequence

3. _____ coordination

4. _____ subordination

5. _____ antecedent

6. _____ tense

7. _____ modifier

8. _____ reflexive pronoun

9. _____ category

10. _____ parenthetic

a. the logical progression of ideas or facts

b. the noun to which a pronoun refers

c. results when all sentences in a paragraph support the topic sentence

d. a word that changes, limits, describes, or explains

e. the compounding or joining of two or more equal language elements

f. does not follow a regular pattern to form its principal parts

g. supplementary of explanatory material not closely related to the rest of the sentence

h. the joining of language elements that are related, but not equal

i. time

j. a group of words related to each other in the same way

k. show that the subject of the sentence is also the object of the verb

Complete these sentences (each answer, 3 points).

11. Four types of sentences are a. _____ , b. _____ ,
    c. _____ , and d. _____ .

12. Three cases of personal pronouns are a. _____ ,
    b. _____ , and c. _____ .

13. The three principal parts of a verb are the a. _____ ,
    b. _____ , and c. _____ .

14. Three forms of intonations are a. _____ ,
    b. _____ , and c. _____ .

15. Apostrophes are used to indicate a. _____ and
    b. _____ .

Capitalize and punctuate where needed (each part, 1 point).

16. when naomi decided to leave moab her daughters in law went with her.

17. after the recitation of lincoln's gettysburg address we all sang my country tis of thee.

Circle the correct word (each answer, 2 points).

18. Won't you (sit / set) over there?

19. What time do you (raise / rise) in the morning?

20. He (lay / laid) in bed all day.

Answer *true* **or** *false* (each answer, 1 point).

21. _____ A sentence that states the main idea in the paragraph is called the
    key sentence.

22. _____ The emphasis or force placed on a spoken word is called *stress*.

23. _____ When you listen to a political speech you should use critical listening.

24. _____ The logical progression of ideas or facts is called chronometric logistics.

25. _____ The word *embarrassed* is correctly spelled.

26. _____ The word *wheather* is correctly spelled.

27. _____ The *s* form of the verb is used in the present tense, third person singular.

28. _____ A verb should agree with its object in person and number.

29. _____ Prepositions may be used as adjectives, adverbs, and conjunctions.

30. _____ The future perfect tense is frequently used.

List these items (each answer, 2 points).

31. List four demonstrative pronouns.

a. _____   b. _____

c. _____   d. _____

32. List four kinds of listening.

a. _____   b. _____

c. _____   d. _____

Match these sentences and sentence patterns (each answer, 2 points).

33. _____ The sixteenth President was Abraham Lincoln.   a. S–V

34. _____ Pamela quickly handed Joe his Bible.   b. S–V–DO

35. _____ Many colorful butterflies flit through the flowers. c. S–LV–PN

36. _____ Charlie quickly placed the glass on the kitchen table.   d. S–LV–PA

e. S–V–IO–DO

Write the letter for the correct answer on each line (each answer, 2 points).

37. What are the principal parts of *to see?* _____
    a. see, sees, saw   b. see, saw, seen
    c. see, seen, seen   d. see, seeing, saw

38. Which sentence uses the past perfect tense of *to read?* _____
    a. I have read the assignment.
    b. I had read the assignment before.
    c. I shall have read the assignment by morning.
    d. I have been reading the assignment.

39. Which sentence is imperative? _____
    a. Can you see the house from here?
    b. Close the door when you leave.
    c. I'll come over there later.
    d. That's quite a large dog!

40. Which sentence contains a prepositional phrase used as an adjective? _____
    a. In the morning we will leave.
    b. I want to go by plane.
    c. The helpful child was very quiet.
    d. The girl with blue eyes is my sister.

ALTERNATE SPELLING TEST

1	agreeable	The gruff, old man was not **agreeable** to our suggestion.	agreeable
2	embarrassed	I was extremely **embarrassed** by his action.	embarrassed
3	grammar	We are studying **grammar** in English.	grammar
4	impatience	My **impatience** is not a good quality.	impatience
5	possessive	The mother had a **possessive** attitude toward her children.	possessive
6	presence	Your **presence** at the meeting is greatly appreciated.	presence
7	receive	To be saved we need to **receive** Christ as our personal Lord.	receive
8	relief	It is a **relief** to know that you are safe.	relief
9	threw	The pitcher **threw** me out at first base.	threw
10	through	Read Matthew, chapters five **through** seven.	through
11	uninterrupted	The teacher spoke on, **uninterrupted**, for three hours.	uninterrupted
12	whether	It does not matter **whether** we go or not.	whether
13	argument	An **argument** is often caused by something relatively unimportant.	argument
14	compel	I cannot **compel** you to follow my instructions.	compel
15	famous	Mark Twain is a **famous** author.	famous
16	finally	Bob **finally** arrived in Japan after days of travel on a freighter.	finally
17	individual	Each **individual** must make his own decision for Christ.	individual
18	label	Read each **label** carefully.	label
19	muscle	Jamie pulled a **muscle** running to third base.	muscle
20	mysterious	We could not explain her **mysterious** disappearance.	mysterious
21	previous	I do not know how the **previous** tenants worked the pump.	previous
22	temple	Jesus said that the **temple** would be destroyed and raised again in three days.	temple
23	woolly	The material had a **woolly** texture.	woolly
24	accent	A word may have different meanings depending on where the **accent** is placed.	accent

ALTERNATE SPELLING TEST

25	accurate	I hope that your information is **accurate**.	accurate
26	adverb	To use an **adverb** correctly we should know its function.	adverb
27	antonym	We had to write an **antonym** for each of ten words.	antonym
28	declarative	We usually write paragraphs with **declarative** statements.	declarative
29	interrogative	A question is an **interrogative** statement.	interrogative
30	peddle	I had to **peddle** furiously to get up the steep hill.	peddle
31	preposition	A **preposition** often relates one word to another.	preposition
32	quotation	"Four score and seven years ago" is a **quotation**.	quotation
33	subject	The king rewarded the loyal **subject**.	subject
34	verb	The **verb** is the action word of a sentence.	verb
35	four	The Olympics are held every **four** years.	four
36	rain	The April **rain** made the air smell fresh.	rain
37	reign	Queen Elizabeth's **reign** was long and powerful.	reign
38	rein	Government officials keep a tight **rein** on the economy.	rein
39	right	Do what is **right** in God's eyes.	right
40	road	The stagecoach bounced wildly down the **road**.	road
41	rode	When father was young, he **rode** a horse to school.	rode
42	sew	Candy learned to **sew** in home economics class.	sew
43	so	Mom will be home soon **so** let us clean up our mess.	so
44	sow	The farmer began to **sow** his crop.	sow
45	threw	Charlie **threw** the ball all the way from the center field fence to home plate.	threw
46	through	Betsy almost walked **through** the arcadia door.	through
47	advertisement	The **advertisement** held my attention.	advertisement
48	appreciate	I **appreciate** the effort you have made on my behalf.	appreciate
49	appropriate	Is that dress **appropriate** apparel for church?	appropriate
50	borrow	It is not wise to **borrow** something and forget to return it.	borrow

ALTERNATE SPELLING TEST

51	creation	God's **creation** was completed in six days.	creation
52	entertainment	Reading is a form of **entertainment**.	entertainment
53	forehead	The ball hit her right in the middle of the **forehead**.	forehead
54	imagination	Pete's vivid **imagination** helped him write exciting stories.	imagination
55	legalize	Many people want to **legalize** prayer in public schools.	legalize
56	opportunity	If I had the **opportunity** to go to Australia, I would take it.	opportunity
57	repetition	The needle of the phonograph stuck causing a **repetition** of the same song.	repetition
58	superstition	The Native American tribe had a **superstition** about the mountain.	superstition
59	cavity	I had a big **cavity** in my front tooth.	cavity
60	effectively	Because of its many side effects, DDT can no longer be used **effectively** against insects.	effectively
61	experience	Have you ever had the **experience** of being lost in the desert?	experience
62	graciously	Timothy **graciously** offered to take his turn last.	graciously
63	legislative	The **legislative** procedures often seem long and drawn out.	legislative
64	musician	I really enjoy the songs of a good **musician**.	musician
65	penetrated	In the Civil War General Sherman **penetrated** the Southern defenses.	penetrated
66	question	Jill only missed one **question** on the test.	question
67	rinse	Mother puts fabric softener in the **rinse**.	rinse
68	stomach	Mother took Susan to the doctor because of the pain in her **stomach**.	stomach
69	urgent	William received an **urgent** message from his brother.	urgent
70	yesterday	We went to the zoo **yesterday**.	yesterday